What Does Your School Data Team Sound Like?

What Does Your School Data Team Sound Like?

A Framework to Improve the Conversation Around Data

Dean T. Spaulding and Gail M. Smith

CORWIN
A SAGE Publishing Company

FOR INFORMATION:

Corwin

A SAGE Company

2455 Teller Road

Thousand Oaks, California 91320

(800) 233-9936

www.corwin.com

SAGE Publications Ltd.

1 Oliver's Yard

55 City Road

London EC1Y 1SP

United Kingdom

SAGE Publications India Pvt. Ltd.

B 1/I 1 Mohan Cooperative Industrial Area

Mathura Road, New Delhi 110 044

India

SAGE Publications Asia-Pacific Pte. Ltd.

3 Church Street

#10-04 Samsung Hub

Singapore 049483

Printed in the United States of America

Library of Congress Cataloging-in-Publication Data

Names: Spaulding, Dean T., author. | Smith, Gail (Gail M.), author.

Title: What does your school data team sound like? : a framework to improve the conversation around data / Dean T. Spaulding and Gail M. Smith.

Description: Thousand Oaks, California : Corwin, 2019. | Includes bibliographical references and index.

Identifiers: LCCN 2018006756 | ISBN 9781506390925 (pbk. : alk. paper)

Subjects: LCSH: Educational evaluation—United States. | Educational indicators—United States. | Education—United States—Data processing. | School improvement programs—United States. | School management and organization—United States—Decision making.

Classification: LCC LB2822.75 .S694 2019 | DDC 379.1/58—dc23

LC record available at https://lccn.loc.gov/2018006756

This book is printed on acid-free paper.

Publisher: Arnis Burvikovs

Development Editor: Desirée A. Bartlett

Editorial Assistant: Eliza Erickson

Production Editor: Jane Martinez

Copy Editor: Gretchen Treadwell

Typesetter: C&M Digitals (P) Ltd.

Proofreader: Caryne Brown

Indexer: Amy Murphy

Cover Designer: Michael Dubowe

Certified Chain of Custody
Promoting Sustainable Forestry
www.sfiprogram.org
SFI-01268

SFI label applies to text stock

18 19 20 21 22 10 9 8 7 6 5 4 3 2 1

Contents

Preface

A s you already know, we, in education, are no strangers to data. It is all around us. In fact, there has never been a time in the history of education when we have had access to more data than right now. But what do we do with all of this data? Sadly, the answer to this question many times is "as little as possible." It seems that the sheer amount of data and the ease of accessing it (e.g., computers, the Internet, online web pages) has not sparked our natural curiosity as educators to engage in education data. Let's face it, we work with data when we have to. We attend (and even participate) in those once-a-year data meetings when the superintendent gathers everyone together to review the results of the most recent state ELA or math assessment. Along with our colleagues we break out into groups to discuss ways in which we can use this data to improve student performance for the next year. But our effort generally stops there.

While this exercise may have good intention, it has more challenges than what could possibly be listed in the space we have for writing this preface. And after the meeting about the test scores, what do we do? Unfortunately, it is "business as usual." People go back to their classrooms to get ready to start the school year and in a couple of days, once the students arrive, all is forgotten . . . until the next year, when the same process is repeated with the exact same results. We have appropriately named them *data days*.

Sadly, data should not be examined once a year but should be examined routinely by a group of dedicated individuals who have a plan in place to capitalize on all that the data has to offer. A data team is just that. Data teams are small groups of three to eight individuals who come together to examine and discuss issues surrounding data and to make programmatic recommendations to improve the issues and problems that they have uncovered. Data teams can also continue to monitor the situation and determine whether or not the actions they have taken have worked.

We are often hired as consultants by school districts to work with data teams at various stages of their development. A couple of years ago we were hired to work with a school building data team at the elementary level. When we asked the school administrator, who hired us, what members of the team wanted us to help them with he replied, "They want to know what an effective data team *sounds* like." Team members not only wanted to know what effective teams sounded like when they discussed data, but they also wanted to know how they could improve the conservations their team was having. Needless to say, we had an extraordinary day working with the team and provided them with a set of strategies to get their conversations back on track.

This experience started us thinking. What did conversations around data sound like? It was an interesting question. How did team members exchange ideas, and was there a difference between teams we found to be effective and those who were less effective? Hence, the genesis of this book began. We hope that reading this book helps improve the conversations around your data team's table. We also hope the conversations never stop but only get better with time.
—D. T. S. & G. S.

CHAPTER OVERVIEWS

Chapter 1. Changing the Lens With the Data Analysis Team (DAT)

The first day your data team meets is one of the most important days. In this chapter, you will be introduced to the data team at Brower Elementary School as they meet for the very first time and hear about all their concerns, questions, and frustrations when it comes to data. The history of school data is overviewed in this chapter, along with how we need to change the lens in which we as educators see data and its role in the overall school improvement process.

Chapter 2. What Should Your Data Team Look Like?

Not all data teams look alike and not all should. The makeup of your data team will depend greatly on your purpose. This chapter will introduce you to different types of teams. There is the mixed team and the nonmixed team approach, each with benefits and challenges. You will also learn how a team functions, to whom the team reports, and how to facilitate effective data team meetings.

Chapter 3. Getting Over the Fear of Data

We all have a fear of data. In this chapter, you and your team members will learn about the basic database and how to construct a simple database. You will also learn about different types of data and how you can work with these different types, and what types of data can be used for what purposes. You will also learn about some nontraditional data sets that you might not have considered using in the past but will find helpful in the future.

Chapter 4. How to Know What Works

In this chapter, you will learn about how research has traditionally determined what works in education and you will be introduced to the improvement cycle, another method used to determine what works. This chapter will provide you with the foundation for the next chapter that unveils two different types of improvement cycles for your DAT to use.

Chapter 5. Following the Steps in the Exploratory and Confirmatory Cycles

This chapter will lead you step-by-step through the exploratory and the confirmatory improvement cycles.

Chapter 6. More Ways to Examine Data

In this chapter, you will learn about different methods of examining data, as well as different methods for displaying data and findings. These methods include line graphs, bar graphs, pie charts, and tables. This chapter also provides a more in-depth perspective of working with baseline data, particularly when baseline data is unstable or inconsistent.

Chapter 7. Collecting Formative Data

Sometimes the data accessible to your data team through the school's archives isn't all the data you and your team members need to draw the right conclusions. Sometimes you need to go out and collect a little more data in order to feel that you have made the right decision. In this chapter, you will learn about different types of data that your data team may be able to collect, as well as establish sound protocols and methods of collecting it. This data may include, but is not limited to, classroom observations, observations of professional development, and surveys.

Chapter 8. Adding Parents to Your DAT

Parents can and should be a part of your data team. The perspective of parents and guardians is very important when examining data and making programmatic decisions in order to promote ongoing school improvement and student success. In this chapter, you will read about some benefits and some challenges when parents are included on the team. There are also some pointers to keep in mind as educators in order to make parents and guardians feel welcome.

Chapter 9. Continuing the Conversation Surrounding Student Data

Each year, thousands of teachers around the country attend meetings to discuss the latest results of student performance. What do these conversations sounds like? Unfortunately, more often than not these conversations are not positive. Traditionally these conversations have been more of a "blame game" rather than a healthy conversation about what to do next to improve student scores on annual, state standardized tests. In this chapter, you will be able to hear the conversations of several data teams who are reviewing their annual state data and strategies about how to approach and use this data to drive programmatic improvements.

Chapter 10. Scaling Up Data

Once your DAT has achieved success with implementing a plan, you will want to start thinking about the best methods for scaling or expanding this practice to other buildings so they too can reap the same rewards. This chapter will provide you with a framework for systematically expanding a project to a new building using best practices. It will provide your DAT with some additional ideas and tips about how to go about working with a new building's DAT in order to achieve success for all.

Acknowledgments

We would like to thank all the hardworking and dedicated educators who volunteer each year to serve on their building's data team. We would also like to thank Amanda Rozsavolgyi for her feedback and technical assistance with preparation of this manuscript. Best wishes. —D. T. S. & G. S.

PUBLISHER'S ACKNOWLEDGMENTS

Corwin gratefully acknowledges the contributions of the following reviewers:

Sandra Enger
Associate Professor and Associate Director of the Institute for Science Education
The University of Alabama
Huntsville, AL

Neil MacNeill
Head Master
Ellenbrook Independent Primary School
Western Australia, Australia

Karen Tichy
Assistant Professor of Educational Leadership
Saint Louis University, School of Education
St. Louis, MO

Bonnie Tryon
Principal for Instructional Planning and Support

Cobleskill-Richmondville Central School
Cobleskill, NY

Rosemarie Young
Field Placement Coordinator, Retired Elementary Principal
Bellarmine University
Louisville, KY

About the Authors

Dean T. Spaulding is the vice president and director of new projects for Z Score Inc., a consulting company that focuses on grant writing, research, and professional development for K–12 and higher education settings. He is the author of several books and coauthor of *Instructional Coaches and the Instructional Leadership Team: A Guide for School-Building Improvement* (Corwin, 2012). He and Gail Smith continue to work with data teams around the country. He can be contacted at Dspaulding@zscore.net

Gail M. Smith is coauthor of *Instructional Leadership Team: A Guide for School-Building Improvement.* Her 36-year career in education included positions as a teacher, assistant principal, assistant superintendent, and deputy superintendent of schools. In 1988, Gail was a finalist for New York State Teacher of the Year. Now retired, Gail travels the world like a true explorer.

Changing the Lens With the Data Analysis Team (DAT)

FIRST DAY OF THE DATA ANALYSIS TEAM

It is 3:30 p.m. and the students at Brower Elementary have all left the building for the day. Teachers pack up their rooms and will shortly follow. Soon the building will be empty except of a small group of six teachers who have gathered at one of the large wooden tables in the back corner of the library. Despite the fact that they have worked together for years they have never come together to serve on a data team before. Because of this they are unsure of many things: their overall purpose, their mission, their responsibilities. There is one thing that they are sure of—that if these sessions became a venue for using data to berate teachers and tell them that they are not doing their jobs, then they are out of there. Let's take a moment and listen in on their conversation. . . .

(Continued)

(Continued)

Jack: Here we go again. Just look at these test scores. I knew we didn't do well but I didn't think it was going to be this bad. Now we have to decide what to do about it.

Christine: Again . . . like we haven't been through this before . . . only every June!

Jack: I hate this, another chance to hear how badly our kids did. We had a good plan last year for how we were going to increase the scores; at least we all thought so, but not good enough I guess.

Christine: Yes, I hate it too, but I feel like this is a little bit different. Our principal, Gabby Neils, asked me to be on what she was calling a DAT: a data analysis team. I didn't have a clue what she meant until she mentioned the test scores. I guess she is just asking a small group to work on the plan instead of the whole faculty.

Klara: Yes, that is what I think this may be too. I wasn't really excited about another chance to hear how we missed the mark, but hey—I like Gabby so I said yes. She's working as hard as we are so I am happy to help her out if I can.

Laura: You know, I had the same thought when she approached me. I said I would do it because I think maybe she might be willing to try a new way of dealing with this. At least I hope so. We can't keep doing this in the same old way as always. It isn't getting us where we want to go! We will see what she has to say.

Jack: Well, she seems pretty open-minded and she has some new ways to look at things so maybe . . .

Emma: I hope we can talk about some other things besides the state test report. I can think of lot of things we probably should consider. I am going to suggest that if she doesn't seem to be headed that way.

Oliver: Okay, but just for the record, I'm out of here if it is the same old same old! I do want to try and look at these results in a deeper way and I also think Beverly, our ELA coordinator, should be invited to help out. She has a lot of information and ideas. I went to her last in-service and it was pretty good. But . . . I am not going to stay on this team if all we do is an endless analysis of those test results. That is okay to begin with, but really, where has it gotten us so far? Been there, done that since I came to this school district!

Laura: Well, I heard that the middle and high schools are also thinking of starting data teams. Maybe we will all work together at some point.

Jack: Okay, I am willing to see where this goes but I have to tell you, the idea of being a data team doesn't strike me as something that will be positive. I also want to know why us? Why did she pick us? I really want an answer to that.

Christine: Exactly. If that is all this is, I say we just take last year's plan, make some adjustments and get on with it. Data—ugh—how I hate that word! I also hate statistics. Remember that class we had to take in graduate school? I hope we don't have to do statistics.

Oliver: Don't you mean sadistics?

Everyone around the table chuckles.

Emma: I wonder where Gabby is. She said she was going to stop in at the first meeting to talk to us and tell us more about what exactly we are supposed to be doing.

Christine: Maybe Gabby will suggest a new way to go. I sure hope so. Our kids need to do better. That is the bottom line for all of this.

Oliver: I hope you are right or, as I said, I am out of here!

Is Data the New Four-Letter Word?

The first place to start with any data team, whether it is new or already in existence, is to determine *what* a data team is. As in the above vignette, we have found that members of a data team often have different perspectives as to what their roles are and what the team's overall mission is. This doesn't mean that everyone has to agree and see things the same way. In fact, a final product is often more meaningful if it is developed through a bipartisan perspective; however, having a data team that does not share the same overall vision can, at times, be counterproductive. So, let's make our first goal to establish a collective definition for a data team. But to do this we first have to have an understanding about data and the historical role data has played in our education system.

If you were to look up the word *data* in the Webster's Dictionary, you would most likely find the following definition:

> factual information (as measurements or statistics) used as a basis for reasoning, discussion, or calculation e.g. the data is plentiful and easily available. (Webster's Unabridged Dictionary)

However, if you were to ask educators to define data you might get this definition:

> A word that has been viewed more in despair than in hope by legions of educators; a word seen more as a weapon than as a useful tool or roadmap by those in the educational field. A word more likely to imprison than to empower unless we decide to learn more about it; its secret clues are there just waiting to be uncovered if only we can find a way to see it in a new, less pejorative light.

When it comes to working with and using data many educators are apprehensive. And can we blame them? In many cases data has been used in education "against" teachers and in doing so has created a difficult situation for many educators to now jump on board and engage with data in any meaningful way.

Our long and painful history with the concept of data has led us to a dead end where the benefits it could provide are masked by the suspicion and negativity it has often brought to schools, teachers, and students. We desperately need to change the conversation, the direction and the narrative, if we are going to be able to use data successfully to improve practice and ultimately improve the learning experience for our students. Professionals and practitioners need to take control of this valuable resource that has become increasingly abundant in recent years, and use data in ways that will shed light on the answers and help us change direction toward academic excellence for all students.

Experts suggest that in order to make this happen we need to change the lens through which data is now seen (Bernhardt, 2005; Thessin, 2015). We need to learn from the stormy history we in education have had with "data" and write a new story—one with a happy ending rather than a repeated plot narrative which sends us back to the start each year.

Experts writing in the field of educational improvement note that at no other time in our history have schools had more data than we do right now (Darling-Hammond, 2010). And at no other time in our history did we do as little as we do now with all of this data (Bernhardt, 2009). In short, we need to find ways to embrace data and make it work for us, rather than against us. To that comment you are probably thinking, "Easier said than done!" To this we simply reply, "We agree, but it can and must be done." You might even counter, "How exactly do you propose that we do that, especially in this era of accountability where the stakes have been increasingly raised for all of us?" "Well," we would respond, "first you need to change the conversation and then determine what data is needed and how to make it work for your school." What follows in these pages is a plan for doing just that: learning more about this potentially powerful diagnostic tool and discovering ways data can be used to truly and meaningfully benefit all the stakeholders.

What we also include in the discussion is a concept that many schools are now embracing: the **data analysis team** (DAT). A DAT is a team of professionals, approximately 3 to 8, who are willing to come together and work collaboratively to review data, determine potential solutions to address problems or issues, and to continue to revisit the data in order to monitor ongoing programming success. We will suggest a process for setting up and running a successful DAT, one that is inclusionary and evidence driven and one that will make best use of the very limited time available to all of you. A DAT is one of the surest ways that we can change the narrative and make data work for us rather than against us.

CHANGING THE LENS FOR HOW WE VIEW DATA

First and foremost, we have to change the way in which most of us see "data." Thus far, much of our experience with data has not been positive; faculties and school communities often see it as a judgment or an indictment of our efforts, our expertise and our success. We need to change that lens, and we believe that a successfully functioning DAT is an excellent way to do exactly that.

We assume that if you picked up this book you are either interested in starting a DAT or have recently started one at your school. Either way, you are curious about data teams and wish to know more. In the next chapter, you will learn about how to successfully set up a DAT and some of the characteristics or frameworks that should be established early on in the process; if you are in those early stages of setting up a DAT, Activity 1 is an excellent way to begin fostering a discussion with educators as well as DAT members regarding data.

ACTIVITY 1

Let us suggest an activity for you personally or for your faculty or DAT. In fact, this might be a good first exercise to do when your data team meets for the very first time. When we start our initial work with data teams, we often do this activity as an icebreaker.

Take two or three minutes and write down one-word responses that come to mind when you hear the word *data*. There are no right or wrong answers—just let it be a free flow. Once you have done that, let's look at what you have written and compare it to responses that we have collected to that same question in various different school settings where we have met to help establish DATs.

Example 1
stick, label, judgment, frustration, dead end, confusing, challenging, vague, a mystery, failure, unfair, numbers, scorecard, pointless, shame, blame game . . .

Example 2
helpful, necessary, inspiring, problem solving, collaborative, engaging, meaningful . . .

Take a moment to inspect your list. Does it look similar to Example 1? If so, you are typical of the responses we have encountered in our initial efforts with DATs as they begin. Yet we have also come to discover that DATs in existence for a while have different and often more positive responses to the concept of data, more similar to Example 2. Why? We believe it is because the lens has been changed; the team members have learned more about all the different types of data and how they measure progress and growth, how data can and should inform decision making, and how to use data as a force for good. Most important, educators have come to realize the connection between data and the success of their students. DATs have found the way to make data work as it was always intended: to increase the levels of academic success for all students, to eliminate unsuccessful efforts, and to build on growth and achievement.

Changing the narrative, changing the lens through which we see data, learning to measure what we need to know, uncovering the clues in the data at hand, taking control and using data as a diagnostic tool as opposed to a sweeping judgment—these are all the tasks for the school's DAT. It is vital that these teams be efficient, credible, knowledgeable, and positive. The members should be those who are most gifted at communication with peers. Creating such successful DATs is the primary goal of this book. It all begins with a successful first meeting. The DAT that starts with a well-organized first meeting is more likely to see their purpose and mission and get down to thoughtful, meaningful work that energizes each member creatively, cognitively, and professionally. A DAT that starts off in less than ideal circumstances (like our friends in the library at Brower Elementary), left to their own accord at their first meeting with no leadership present to help set the stage and guide them, is unfortunately more likely to crash and burn unless they don't get on track quickly.

WHERE DID ALL THIS DATA COME FROM?

There is one thing that everyone agrees on. We are surrounded in education by data—so much that the sheer amount of data the data teams now have access to is often seen as a barrier. In fact, one of the first challenges many data teams face is where to begin. We thus present Activity 2, which we recommend every data team (especially those that are new and unsure where to start) use. It will not only get the creative juices flowing, but will serve the team well in opening up many data possibilities for which the team might not have otherwise been aware. With so much data out there, the DAT is really the "filter" that examines the different data sources, integrates the data to identify need, and then uses the data to guide and monitor action or change (see Figure 1.1).

Figure 1.1   Overview of DATS

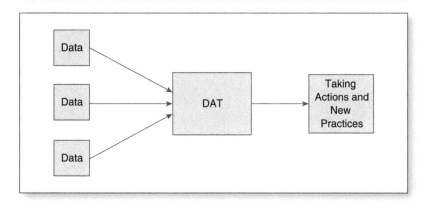

ACTIVITY 2

This is another activity that might also be good to use on one of the first DAT meetings. Ask the team to brainstorm about all the different types of data found in their school building. This is a brainstorming exercise, so the most important part of this process is to make it exhaustive. So the list can (and should) include everything from "number of days students are tardy" to "student scores on that year's state ELA assessment." It is best if people write their data points on individual pieces of paper, or better yet, sticky notes. Place these notes on a wall where everyone can see them. Next, begin to arrange the notes into one of three categories: (1) classroom, (2) building, and (3) system/accountability. *Classroom data* is exactly as it sounds. This is data collected in a classroom setting—everything from attendance, to quiz grades, to number of homework assignments completed. Building data is data that exists outside of the classroom efforts. In other words, an individual teacher isn't in charge or responsible for this data. *Building data* could be anything from daily student attendance at school to student performance on a math assessment that has been developed and administered two times during the school year to monitor students' growth and learning. This type of data should

(Continued)

(Continued)

not be confused with the data collected annually on students' performance from the state. That data is more commonly referred to as *system* or *accountability data*. It is summative in nature in that a final decision is made. In the case of state ELA and math data, a final decision is made about the school, its teachers, and its students.

Once you have the data in the three separate categories, you can start to plan how you will move forward. What type of data is your team interested in? Is this data at all related to other data from another column? Many times what we find is that data from one column will be related to data in another column. Use this visual to spark rich conversations. Be sure to have a member of the team take notes.

One message that will become very clear from participating in Activity 2 is that there is no data too small or insignificant to be excluded from the list. In the midst of the barrage, educators often stop and ask some form of that question, thinking there must have been a time when data wasn't a part of our lives. In truth, data in many forms has always been a part of the modern day educational process. We have always had standardized tests (remember the IOWAs?) and teacher-made tests and state tests. We collected attendance data, drop-out numbers, and other data considered relevant to doing our very best in the teaching and learning process. Data was important then, but in our collective memory, it wasn't the menacing specter it is now to many in our field. When and why did that happen?

In truth it was a slow process. The teaching and learning process always included an effort to look and learn from the data at hand, but the focus began to change in the late 70s and early 80s. Studies published on the effectiveness of our education system began to use data in a big way to point out the shortcomings, the failures, and the inequities. The National Commission on Excellence in Education report, "A Nation at Risk" rang alarm bells throughout the nation. People began to pay attention in specific and focused ways they never had before. The calls for educational excellence and accountability grew louder and louder, demanding action. Serious researchers in our field began to publish studies identifying the correlates found in effective schools. The work of people like Larry Lazotte and Ron Edmonds, for example, was embraced by schools as they began to work in new ways to improve their schools' efforts to educate all students.

Schools became inundated with data at levels never seen before, and not long into the process, states began formalized reports, based on data from sources that included state standardized testing programs and that identified successful schools and "Schools In Need of Improvement." At first these labels either elevated or denigrated a school community, but came with only generalized requirements for those designated as "failing." Faculties scrambled, in the midst of disheartening headlines, to write formal improvement plans devoted to getting their schools off "The List." As these labels were seen to have been the result of the data collected, the gradual change in perception was inevitable. Data became the judgment and slowly went from being seen as helpful and hopeful to being awaited with dread each spring. Educators were expected to "do something" about what this data uncovered, but had little training in what different types of data could demonstrate and how to use it most effectively to improve instruction.

As this process continued, it was inevitable that school success and accountability would become a political issue. No Child Left Behind (NCLB) did that for all fifty states. There is a lot to be grateful for with NCLB, but it is also clear that it needs to be reexamined, modified, and adjusted to achieve all it intended. NCLB can be celebrated for helping us to disaggregate scores, thus ensuring that we have a clear picture of the success of our efforts for *all* students. It also helped to shine a bright light on the needs, truths, and myths about special education; however, it came with additional calls for accountability, providing data to a general public unschooled in all the subtleties within the numbers. The slow decline in our positive view of "data" began to speed up. In our rush to do better and to be better, there were a lot of casualties. Debates raged, and still do, over the value of "snapshot" data versus "growth measures" data, the assumptions of a level playing field and the ability of the tests to measure what we expected them to measure.

The call for teacher accountability is a valid one. We in education do not want to harbor anyone's ineffectiveness, and we want our talents and achievements recognized. However, once again, the demand for measures to define educational excellence and "our" failures has led to a system that is seen by all as in need of retooling. In education, we always have to adjust as we go and the accountability movement has been no exception. The systems in place initially have seemed heavy-handed and cumbersome to many, and data has been assigned the role of villain once again. However, there is hope on the horizon as states begin to tailor these processes and create a system that is both objective and fair.

The good news is that the news is not all bad. Teachers and faculties everywhere are using data-based decision making more than ever to determine successful strategies to implement in schools and classrooms. Action research is a major focus in school communities, and a wider range of stakeholders are looking at what data has to tell us: parents, students, and community have heard more about data in ways both positive and negative than they ever did before. Educators are learning more every day on different types of sources of data, how to use it to inform their efforts, what each source of data does and does not tell us, and how it can point the way to the destination we want to reach. It has led to the formation of Data Analysis Teams who strive to use data as a diagnostic tool, and in doing so, offer the best hope for changing the pejorative lens through which it is seen today.

Okay, Let's Change the Lens!

With data, as with all things, perception is everything. Perception is reality. The lens through which we see "data" determines, to a great extent, whether it can help us or hinder us. The context in which we receive data depends upon our perception of what it means and what it has done and will do to us and for us. For a long time now, the perception the educational community has had of so-called data has been that of an answer to the question: "How did we do?" The "lens" through which we see and examine data has been a single focus lens, measuring our end result and assigning a label of success or failure to that result. Teachers' perception has often, but not always, been one of a judgment, a demand, and an evaluation. Administrators have traditionally seen data as a signpost indicating whether or not their schools are on the right track or the wrong road. Both groups see data as a suggestion for course correction for the following year. Communities usually see only a brief summary of the data at hand and often as a way of knowing whether or not they can be proud of the "good schools" or concerned about "failure" on the most general level. For all groups, data is usually seen as that final word on the success or failure of the school year—cause for celebration or a call to action.

SUMMARY

As we travel further down the road of accountability, in our heartfelt desire to ensure that all our students achieve success, we have focused on data in new ways, looking at many more sources of information than ever before. We have established faculty teams to study data and find ways to make it work more successfully for us. Data Analysis Teams are one of the positive results of this collective "soul searching." We need to continue in our efforts to change and enlarge the conversation surrounding data and to do so, we must first change, or at least adjust, the lens through which we see all this information.

Data can no longer be seen as just a measure of "How did we do?" We need to find ways to use data, which is evidence, to answer different questions as well. We need to ask, "How are we doing at this moment?" several times during the school year. We need to stop and look around and ask, "Are we headed in the right direction?" several times during the year. We need to ask the "who," "what," "where," "when," and, most important, the "why" questions. We need to collectively look at data as a way to tell us "How do we know where we need to go?" and "What important steps are missing in our process?" as well as "Is what we are doing today helping us get where we want to go?" We need to adjust the lens so that we see data as a greater part of the answers to these questions, to allow it to become a day-to-day part of our school's GPS!

Teachers, administrators, and parents can change the conversation and make data work for them. We can change the perceptions, adjust the lens, and take control of the process for data-based decision making and the accountability that follows. Data does not have to be a "four-letter word." It can become synonymous with evidence. It can take its place in our arsenal of diagnostic tools in ways that will lead to the excellence the accountability movement strives for. Changing the lens is not easy, not without it challenges and obstacles, but it can be done.

What Should Your Data Team Look Like?

A week later the DAT at Brower Elementary meets again in the library. This time their principal, Gabby Neils, joins them. Let's take a moment to listen in on their conversation. . . .

Principal
Gabby Neils:

Okay . . . Thanks so much for agreeing to be a part of this, especially since I haven't had the chance to explain my ideas to you until now. I want to apologize again for not being able to make the first meeting. I had an emergency meeting with the superintendent. I also want to clearly state from the beginning that I promise you this won't be business as usual for our process this year even though our task is the same—developing a plan for improvement based on our data and setting our yearly goals. I hope, however, that what we do will be broader in scope and the process much more expanded. The process used to be reading and dissecting the state report and talking with colleagues before writing and implementing our plan. We will still do that but in a different, hopefully more expansive, informed and empowered way. How? First by deciding what questions we really need to ask beyond the obvious ones. Then we will first search the traditional data for answers to our questions, but not just the usual data. Of course, we will examine and study our state formal test results report, but that will only be our starting point. After all, we need to look at ALL the possible sources of information we have, which should also be considered data. How are we now going to define "data"? Well, I think it is simply all the informative and relevant evidence available, and we have a lot more evidence to consider in addition to the state report. Once we have found all the data we need, then—and only then—we can set about the process of following that data to the logical conclusions about what needs to be done. The data is not our report card. It is our investigative tool, our GPS, our evidence. I hope that by the time we have become skilled at this ongoing process you will agree with me.

Okay, this is a lot to throw at you all at once. Let's see what questions you have about all of this.

Oliver: *Sounds interesting but how do we know what information we need?*

Principal Neils: *First, we will brainstorm about what questions we really need to ask and then see what evidence we believe will help get us the answers.*

Laura: *Are we going to use all the data we decide to collect at once? That would be overwhelming I think.*

Jack: *Doesn't sound like it. I think maybe this way we won't need all the information at the same time so I guess the first question I would suggest we ask is "What do we need to know and when?" I think we need some sort of timeline as we move along.*

Klara: Yes, I agree with all that but there is such a thing as too much information, right?

Principal Neils: True, but one of our tasks will be to discard the information or data that doesn't seem to help us to focus.

Christine: I can think of a lot of ideas already about the information we will need. I've believed for years that our attendance data, for example, can tell us more about our ELA weaknesses than we realize.

Principal Neils: Perhaps you're right, Christine. Once we gather all the questions we want to ask, then next will come another session to brainstorm data sources. I hope you will all ask your colleagues for ideas at that point!

Emma: Some of the data we need might even be information that we don't have, but we can figure out where to look.

Christine: I hope there's no statistics!

Principal Neils: Exactly, Emma! I hope this new DAT process will be expansive and that we will welcome new stakeholders to the process. I believe there is a role for students and parents on our team. I'd like you to think about that as we move forward.

Oliver: This all sounds great. Well, maybe not great, but definitely a new idea and I am willing to stay on for now. But if I feel like this becomes the same old judgment and apology process for us—the "We failed and we are sorry" data bashing—I'm not sure I can go through that again. Just being honest. I don't want to hear how we are a failure any more.

Principal Neils: I promise you, Oliver, I'll do everything in my power to make sure that doesn't happen, and I want you to tell me if you think we are headed in

> *that direction. I don't want that either. That's why I want us to take control of our own information, our own data, and make it work FOR us before others decide how we should proceed. Please just promise me that you will tell me if this starts to feel like a negative experience, and I'll do all I can to turn it around. I need your expertise and your voice and your insights.*
>
> Oliver: *Well okay. I guess it is worth a try at least!*
>
> Jack: *So, this is so much to take in. What happens first?*
>
> Principal Neils: *Well I'd like not to be the DAT leader so we need someone willing to at least colead with me. Please consider taking on that role and let me know if you are interested. For now, since we all have the state data, let's do exactly what I suggested and use it to start off. What does it tell us and what questions do we have? Let's begin making a list of questions. If you come up with more before our next meeting, please email them to me. Also, please ask your colleagues for their questions.*
>
> *Let's begin making that list. Who has one they would like to add?*

As we discussed in the previous chapter, data teams have been one thing to come out of the data movement. Like people, data teams come in all shape and sizes. While there are many different compositions for a data team, it is important for the team's makeup to be aligned with its overall purpose.

MIXED VERSUS NONMIXED DATA TEAMS

One way to think about the purpose of your DAT is in how your DAT is organized. In other words, *who* makes up the team is very important and certainly plays a role in its ability to function, as well as how it can function. For example,

Figure 2.1   Mixed Level Data Team

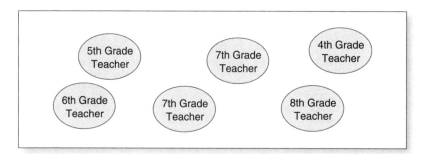

if the purpose of a team is to examine some aspect of student performance across time then a **mixed level team** would be necessary and most effective (Spaulding & Falco, 2010). This design would utilize a team of teachers from different grade levels (e.g., third, fourth, fifth, and sixth grades) (as shown in in Figure 2.1).

One of the benefits of the mixed level team is that it allows one to ask questions of the data from multiple perspectives, as well as create questions that examine the data across time. For example, this type of team could answer the question: What do students need to know in mathematics in sixth, seventh, and eighth grade?

Mixed teams do not only have to consist of teachers. A mixed team could consist of other stakeholder groups (e.g., parents, staff, administration) and in some cases even students. Imagine having student perspectives on what they learned, and how they transition from one grade level to the next as part of the discussions. Certainly this would create an even more diverse perspective of the data.

Another type of team is the **nonmixed level team**. This team consists of participants who are all from the *same* stakeholder group (see Figure 2.2). An example of this type of team would be a data team that consists of *only* sixth grade teachers. Unless team members had taught at other grade levels earlier on in their careers, they would only have a sixth grade perspective. The benefit of this type of team is that it

Figure 2.2   Nonmixed Level Data Team

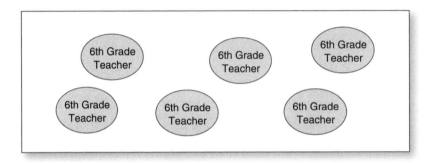

allows the team to dig much deeper into the sixth grade data. Team members would have in-depth knowledge about the interracial components of both formative day-to-day assessments in the classroom, as well as summative assessment such as the annual state test. Team members would know specific things about sixth grade. For example, they would know particular challenges that "creep" up in the curriculum as the year goes on and how they modify instruction along the way to critically address those issues; they would know what issues students struggle with in the beginning of the year and what to look for; they would know what students enjoy most about the classes, lessons, and activities; they could "judge" if things are going well in the class or if they are not, and what they are going to do in order to get the class back on track.

GOALS OF THE DATA TEAM

Establishing several goals early on for the data team is imperative to its overall success. Why? Having a shared vision will allow the team to construct a particular framework around the data and the data analysis process. Without such a vision, the data analysis could be executed in a haphazard manner, which in the end will not produce the results the team had originally intended. You can start out by asking the simple question: What is the purpose of this data team?

Here are some typical responses:

- "To collect and look at data."
- "To improve student learning."
- "To look for trends in data that we couldn't see other-wise."
- "To look at areas that need to be improved upon and then monitor our progress."

In fact, all of the above statements are true. But ultimately, if your DAT is going to be effective and accomplish its goals it is going to have to streamline its investigation and this requires the team to focus on one or two questions. To do this there needs to be agreement, and to have agreement there must be effective communication with everyone having a par-ticular role and responsibility.

WHAT ARE THE ROLES AND RESPONSIBILITIES OF EACH TEAM MEMBER?

Not only is it important to have set goals for the data team, but it is also equally important that each member of the data team knows what their responsibilities to the team are. One way to manage everyone's shared responsibilities is to have a set schedule for meeting times. A data team that establishes a set schedule for meeting is much more productive than those that meet when there is a sudden emergency. To make it easier, many times teams will meet after school the first Monday of every month. It might also be advantageous for each member of the team to have dif-ferent positions. For example, one member might be the director responsible for setting up the agenda for members of the team to discuss. Another member might be respon-sible for physically pulling together the different data and assembling those materials for the team to discuss. Another might serve as notetaker, keeping careful minutes of each data team meeting.

How Will Meetings Be Facilitated?

Ultimately how the data team decides to run its meetings is entirely up to the team. However, there are some characteristics of successful data team meetings to consider for creating the most effective team possible. It is important to set an agenda, and as part of that agenda the main activity the team will be engaging in. In some cases, meetings may consist of team members talking about what "patterns" they see in the data. These patterns may be for individual students or entire classes. At other times the team may need to decide what set of actions need to be taken as a result of the analysis and discussion. Overall, data team meetings are a combination of analysis, discussion, action, and reflection.

It is important to be able to determine if the DAT is operating in a successful manner, but in the midst of all the challenges, tasks, and information, how exactly can we know what an effective DAT sounds like? It is not ever easy, nor is it always clear to know how to answer that question.

If you want your DAT to have productive conversations, here are some suggestions:

1. All participants are listeners and speakers.

2. The topic under discussion is focused and free from tangential considerations.

3. Each team member's contributions are heard and validated.

4. Team leadership is shared. It is facilitative, not autocratic.

5. Negativity is minimized and replaced with serious, scholarly investigation of data.

6. Successes are acknowledged and celebrated. Areas still in need of improvement are recognized and addressed with facts in order to make necessary midcourse corrections.

7. The tone is cordial, respectful, positive, and professional.

8. The efforts and progression are logical in nature.

9. The presence of trust among all members is evident.

10. Setbacks are not received with discouragement, but rather accepted as new data to be examined and understood.

PREPARATION, THE KEY TO SUCCESS

Make sure members of the team do their homework and come prepared. Students are not the only ones with homework that needs to be done. Many times data team members will have homework—data and materials that have to be carefully reviewed and examined prior to the monthly data team meeting. It is important that each member of the team take this responsibility seriously and properly prepare for the meetings. If members of the team come into the data team meeting "cold" without having examined the data, the conversations and rich discussions that are a product of this overall process will be severely impacted. It is also advisable for team members to take notes as they are preparing for the meeting so that they stay focused and on topic, and so their comments clearly align to the data. Here are six suggestions for your DAT:

1. *Block off a certain amount of time for your DAT meeting.* Try to keep meetings short. One hour in length works best and try not to get sidetracked with idle conversations that are off topic. Many times teachers use this time as a platform to talk about "how they teach" and "what they do in the classroom." While this discussion on instruction may be important, it usually doesn't apply to data teams in the sense that the data being examined is looking at aspects on a much larger scale than what one teacher did in his or her classroom on a certain day of the year. If you say the DAT meetings

will be an hour and you hold to that hour, people will be much more likely and energetic in attending them, knowing that it will truly only be an hour.

2. *If you bring food or refreshments serve them after the meeting.* This provides a nice reward for a job well done.

3. *Set an agenda for the meeting.* If your meeting is set for an hour in length then you should have no more than two or three items on the agenda. Also be sure to have "new" and "old" business items on your agenda. This will help build continuity or a connection between meetings, and people will say "Oh yes, this is what we did last time." Also, make sure the agenda goes out to all members of the DAT three to four days in advance. It will remind everyone that there is a data meeting coming up and will start them thinking about what they are going to do at the meeting.

4. *Establish some method for disseminating materials.* Many times materials and information are updated, especially today when we have such quick and immediate access to data. Therefore, make sure that you have some mechanism in place that allows for quick updating of materials and resources and easy access to those updates for all team members. A shared drive is a great way to facilitate this, allowing members to post information, and notifications go out to other members altering them that there have been changes to the originally posted materials. Shared drives are also beneficial in that every member can be instructed to download the final materials onto a laptop or a mobile device, or print them out (whichever works best for them), and bring their own set of materials to the meeting.

5. *How do teams function?* The DAT must function in ways that distinguish it from other traditional faculty groups, teams, or committees. The central goal of the honest and thorough examination of all relevant data

in order to map out the best plan to achieve success at the high levels must always be the focus of the DAT. Essential to success is their willingness to put aside preconceived notions, judgments, and pessimism and to approach this new endeavor with an eye to academic integrity; exploratory rigor; and open, honest, and effective communication with all stakeholders.

ACTIVITIES

1. Starting off on the right foot is a key component for a successful DAT. Early on in your DAT process, give the questions provided on the DAT Activity Sheet to each team member and have them respond in writing. Ask each team member bring their responses to the next DAT meeting and have an open dialogue surrounding the various responses.

2. As you can see from reading this chapter, a DAT can be taken off course quite easily. As a group, brainstorm about possible challenges that the DAT may encounter in the future and the barriers these challenges will create. After you have completed a list of possible challenges, post each one on the board and have team members hypothesize how the DAT might address them. Use the Forecasting Stormy Skies Activity Sheet to help facilitate the responses among team members.

SUMMARY

Understanding the mission and purpose of your DAT is important, but understanding the makeup of your team and who should be on your team is equally important. Not all DATs are the same. Depending on the work, your DAT may decide to select individuals to serve on the team who have different experiences and perspectives. A nonmixed team is a DAT with all the same type of members. For example, it could comprise all sixth-grade teachers. This will allow the DAT to drill down in-depth on different subject matter regarding data for sixth grade. A mixed team consists of members from different grade levels and or content areas. It might also include stakeholders such as parents, staff, or even students. While the mixed team doesn't allow for the concentrated expertise in a particular area, it does allow for extended discussions around the data as students progress from grade to grade and flow through the school system. DATs should not automatically have a school administrator (e.g., a building principal) on the DAT without giving it serious consideration since having an administrator on the team may influence members. It might be best to have a regularly scheduled meeting with a school administrator instead.

DAT ACTIVITY SHEET

Directions: Read the following questions and, in as many words as you need, respond in writing. Be ready and willing to share your thoughts and responses with the team.

1. *What is the goal of our data team?*

2. *What are the roles and responsibilities of each team member?*

3. *How will meetings be facilitated?*

4. *What process or methodology will be followed in using data to make decisions?*

5. *Whom do we report our findings to?*

6. *What actions should be taken based on our findings?*

7. *What are short-term, intermediate-term, and long-term activities and goals for the team?*

FORECASTING STORMY SKIES

Directions: Read each question below and respond in writing accordingly. Be prepared to share your responses collectively with your DAT members.

1. No matter how much you and your DAT plan, inevitably you are going to face some challenges. Take a few minutes and in the space below list some possible challenges or barriers that you foresee your DAT facing as you work toward the future.

2. Reexamine the list of possible challenges and barriers above. Take each one, and in the space below, describe how these challenges can be overcome.

Be prepared to share your challenge forecast and solutions during a team discussion.

Getting Over
the Fear of Data

It is the third meeting of Brower Elementary School DAT. The DAT has decided to forgo having Principal Gabby Neils on their team full time. Instead, they have opted to have her visit periodically to share their findings and where they plan to go as far as recommendations for practice are concerned. Jack has volunteered to serve as the team's leader, and everyone is delighted to have him. He has been a teacher with the district for many years and brings with him experience of testing, students, community, and politics. Now the team is faced with better defining their purpose and their next steps. Let's take a listen to the conversation. . . .

Jack: Okay, folks, here we are again. It was nice for Principal
           Neils to join us last week, but now it comes down to
           what are we going to do at these meetings. The food
           that everyone brings in is great, but at some point we
           need to set our sights on something and go for it.

Christine: What I gathered from our last meeting is that we need
           to find some issues in the building and start looking
           at data on them. I put out a call to the district's data

           (Continued)

(Continued)

person John Healy, who said that he is swamped right now with getting reports to the board of education but would be happy to help us and work with us on the data analysis. So, the good news is we don't have to do statistics!

Laura: So does anyone have any areas where they think we need to be looking?

Oliver: I mean, it doesn't come as a shock to any of us at this table, but we could certainly improve our literacy scores. Especially fifth graders. The last time I looked at the scores I thought that over the last couple of years fifth grade had continued to decline on the state's ELA assessment, while third and fourth grades had maintained. They weren't great either, but at least they hadn't dropped like those of fifth grade.

Kara: Really, I thought fifth grade last year had made some gains because of the new program we had put in place. . . .

Emma: I thought so too, and that fourth and third grade had unfortunately begun to slip.

Laura: I'm not sure, so that is certainly some data that we would want to request from the district's data person.

Jack: That sounds good, but then what? What do we do with this data? What are we trying to see with this data that will drive us in some sort of way to address it?

Christine: These are all good questions. I was so relieved that we didn't have to do statistics, I really forgot to ask about the overall framework or plan we should be using.

Jack: Okay, let me talk to the principal again and see what she was thinking about. Once we understand the overall process I think we will have no trouble moving forward.

Kara: Great, sounds like a plan. Now who wants some of my homemade chocolate chip cookies?

Fear of Data

One challenge that we have to overcome when working with data is fear. At some point, perhaps in an undergraduate or graduate statistics class, we developed a belief that we didn't like data. We developed a belief that we weren't good at data. We believed that working with data was impossible and a real challenge. This is just simply not true. Everyone can be good at working with data. Like everything, it just takes time, practice, and reflection. Yes, at times data can be challenging, but it can also be exciting, liberating, and fun to work with once you get used to it and start to understand it better.

As discussed earlier, schools have more data now than at any other time in history. We also discussed earlier why this has been seen by some as a negative; however, the good news is that the increased emphasis on data has also brought about a new position. These days most districts have one or more data analytics personnel on staff. While they will vary from district to district, the main duties for these individuals is to send data to the state in order to remain in compliance, develop internal data reports for the board of education, and assist others in the district with any data needs that are required. If your district has such a person, then the DAT should reach out to that individual early on. Again, it is recommended that this data person not be part of the regular DAT but could certainly be invited to a meeting now and then to provide insight into the depth and breadth of the data the district currently collects. The DAT should also establish a process with the district's data person to request data sets.

What Is a Data Set?

A **data set** is a collection of individual data points that have meaning. A data set is not just one piece of data (e.g., an individual student's reading score), but a collection of individual points or pieces of data (e.g., the individual reading scores for an entire class, grade level, a school building, district, or region).

Exhibit 3.1   A Simple Data Set

65, 100, 87, 77, 69, 98, 85, 66, 100, 99, 50, 44, 100, 43, 87, 92, 69, 84

Exhibit 3.1 presents an example of a simple data set for a sixth grade classroom and each student's score on a mathematics quiz. This is a data set because it "holds" many pieces of data.

WHAT IS A DATABASE?

A data set and a database have similarities and differences. A data set generally contains one variable. For example, the data set presented in Exhibit 3.1 only focuses on students' math scores. A database, however, is a term that is used to refer to set of data that contains multiple variables for a set of individuals. Table 3.1 presents an example of a basic database found in education.

Take a moment to review the database in Table 3.1 What are things that we are able to talk about from this database? First of all, there are five variables (six, if you count the Student ID) in this database: gender, ethnicity, grade, special education, and free or reduced lunch. We typically refer to these five variables as demographic data. Demographics describe the subjects of students in a database. For example, if the student is female or male, what ethnicity he or she is, and whether the student is in special education or receiving a free or reduced lunch. One can get a lot of information about those in the database just from the demographics alone!

In addition to demographics, we can have other forms of data that summarize a student across the entire school year on a particular variable or outcome measure. In the case of the database presented in Table 3.2, the time period is for the entire school year and the variables are focused on student behavior.

After examining the behavior database, what kinds of questions can we generate? We can certainly see that some students have had more issues during the school year than others (e.g., Student ID 54655).

Table 3.1   Basic Database

Student ID	Gender	Ethnicity	Grade	Special Education	Free or Reduced Lunch
5430343	F	W	10	Yes	Yes
5664533	F	A	10	No	Yes
454323	M	B	10	No	No
434544	M	B	10	No	No
54655	F	W	10	No	No
542234	M	B	10	Yes	Yes
542445	F	A	10	No	No
323452	M	W	10	Yes	Yes
453424	F	W	10	No	No

Table 3.2   Student Behavior Database

Student ID	Total Office Referrals	Total Suspensions	Total Days Absent	Total Tardy
5430343	2	1	5	1
5664533	0	0	0	3
454323	10	9	32	20
434544	1	0	3	2
54655	15	10	30	2
542234	0	0	3	0
542445	0	0	0	0
323452	3	4	2	1
453424	1	1	10	10

The third database, presented in Table 3.3, selects variables that are focused on student academic achievement.

Table 3.3   Student Academic Database

Student ID	GPA	SAT Score	State ELA Raw Score	State ELA Level	State Math Raw Score	State Math Level
5430343	3	800	499	3	500	3
5664533	5	1590	699	4	698	4
454323	2	630	380	2	400	2
434544	2	700	385	2	402	2
54655	3	803	502	3	500	3
542234	1	599	400	1	403	1
542445	5	1580	699	4	720	4
323452	4	1500	600	4	602	4
453424	1	600	400	1	410	2

In the student academic database, we can see the different outcomes related to academic achievement by Student ID.

Kept separate these databases are somewhat limited in what they can do for us, as well as in the depth and breadth of the questions they are able to answer; however, if all three of these databases (i.e., demographics, behavior, and academics) are merged into one large database, the number of questions it can now answer is greatly expanded.

Now, take a look at Table 3.4; with all of the sixteen variables combined. What types of complex questions could you now ask of the data? For example, one could ask the question: Is there any difference between males and females in students who performed on the SAT? Or, are there any relationships between the number of days a student is absent and the number of disciplinary referrals? Take a moment and see how many questions you can generate. We will revisit the art of developing questions later on in this book, but for now let's talk about some basic aspects of a database.

Table 3.4 Example of Expanded Database

Student ID	Gender	Ethnicity	Grade	Special Education	Free or Reduced Lunch	GPA	SAT Score	State ELA Raw Score	State ELA Level	State Math Raw Score	State Math Level	Total Office Referrals	Total Suspensions	Total Days Absent	Total Tardy
5430343	F	W	10	Yes	Yes	3	800	499	3	500	3	2	1	5	1
5664533	F	A	10	No	Yes	5	1590	699	4	698	4	0	0	0	3
454323	M	B	10	No	No	2	630	380	2	400	2	10	9	32	20
434544	M	B	10	No	No	2	700	385	2	402	2	1	0	3	2
54655	F	W	10	No	No	3	803	502	3	500	3	15	10	30	2
542234	M	B	10	Yes	Yes	1	599	400	1	403	1	0	0	3	0
542445	F	A	10	No	No	5	1580	699	4	720	4	0	0	0	0
323452	M	W	10	Yes	Yes	4	1500	600	4	602	4	3	4	2	1
453424	F	W	10	No	No	1	600	400	1	410	2	1	1	10	10

35

ARCHIVAL DATA

For most cases, the DAT will be given access to data that is already collected and will not require any effort from DAT members themselves to collect. Data that is already collected by someone else other than those who are analyzing it is referred to as **archival data**. While one of the benefits of using archival data is the ease in obtaining it, the barrier to its use is the fact that those who are analyzing it do not know the accuracy or validity with which it was collected. One has to assume that standard procedures were in place and used when the data was collected. For example, for the question involving students' SAT scores one would have to function under the assumption that when students took their SATs at the various testing locations that those testing sites followed the standardized procedure for administering the assessment. Unfortunately, there is little one can do to confirm the authenticity of the data and so must use the data believing that it has been collected in good faith.

SETTING UP A DATABASE

When setting up a database there are some common rules or guidelines to adhere to. The first rule is that each case or subject (e.g., student) is represented in the database in rows. If you have 50 students, then you also have 50 rows in your database with each row representing a student. (Actually, you have 51 rows if you have the first row with labels across each column.) While subjects are rows, variables are represented by columns. This is the framework for all databases.

The space where row meets column is referred to as a *cell*. Individual pieces of data that correspond to the subject and the variable go into a single cell. For example, for Student ID 5430343, her SAT score is 800. The score 800 is occupying a cell. The important thing to remember is only one piece of data can occupy that particular cell. The SAT score for Student ID 5664533 is found in the cell beneath it, thus corresponding to another student.

Summing or adding up data is one way to go about analyzing data. We typically sum data by totaling up columns. Continuing with the example, we would get a sum or total of days absent by totaling up the Total Days Absent Column. In this case the answer would be 85 Total Days Absent across all nine students.

There are many statistical software products on the market that can perform analysis at a click of a button (literally!). Statistical Package for the Social Sciences (IBM® SPSS® Statistics), R, and Statistical Analysis System (SAS®) are some common examples. Excel is an electronic spreadsheet that may prove very useful to you and your DAT members. One of the benefits of Excel is that it is often part of word processing packages (i.e., the Microsoft Office Suite) that many people already have available to them on their computers. In addition, Excel is a powerful spreadsheet that allows one to conduct a wide variety of applications and analyses of the data. It should be noted that this book is not designed to be a guide to using Excel or any software package. For further in-depth information, we recommend that you obtain a manual or guide specifically for the data software you select; however, in this book we will touch upon some basic skills and will use Excel to demonstrate those skills as a point of reference.

ENTERING DATA CORRECTLY IN A CELL

A cell can have only one bit or piece of information. If there is more than that entered into a cell one will not be able to perform the desired analysis. This is probably best conveyed by showing an example of where this idea is violated. Take for example Table 3.5. In this situation, the office referrals have been recorded for each quarter of the school year; however, instead of giving each quarter its own cell, all four quarters are entered into a cell, separated by commas.

This is an incorrect way to enter data into a database because it will not allow one to easily manipulate it or analyze it in any way. One cannot simply highlight the column and sum it. To correct this there should only be one piece of data

Table 3.5   Student Office Referrals by Quarter Database

Student ID	Number of Referrals Q1, Q2, Q3, Q4
5430343	3, 0, 5, 1
5664533	0, 0, 0, 0
454323	3, 1, 0, 9
434544	3, 2, 4, 1
54655	0, 0, 0, 1
542234	1, 0, 1, 0
542445	2, 1, 0, 0
323452	0, 0, 2, 1
453424	9, 0, 0, 1

Table 3.6   Student Office Referrals by Quarter Database

Student ID	Q1	Q2	Q3	Q4
5430343	3	0	5	1
5664533	0	0	0	0
454323	3	1	0	9
434544	3	2	4	1
54655	0	0	0	1
542234	1	0	1	0
542445	2	1	0	0
323452	0	0	2	1
453424	9	0	0	1
Total	21	4	12	14

in each cell, and therefore each quarter assigned to its own column—four columns in total, plus one column for Student ID. In Table 3.6 this has been corrected.

Now one can easily sum each column and determine the total number of office referrals for each quarter.

LEVELS OF DATA

If you have ever taken an educational research or statistics course, you probably remember the professor discussing the different types of data at some point in the class. All data—whether from end-of-year assessments, classroom data, or school records—fits into one of four different types of categories. These categories are: (1) categorical, (2) ordinal, (3) interval, and (4) ratio. One question that many people have is why this is important. Why do I need to know the different levels of data? The answer is because the type of data dictates the type of analysis one can perform on the data. Unfortunately, not all data is created equal, which means it is necessary for you to identify which level data you are working with in order to perform the best or correct analysis. Let's take a moment to discuss each one of these and give some examples to help clarify. Let's start with the simplest and move up.

Categorical data is the simplest level of data but still very important to the data analysis process. Think of categorical data as data that puts things into distinct "boxes." Educational data is filled with categorical data. For example, gender is categorical because it places subjects into two boxes, "male" or "female," as we have seen in the databases described earlier. Categorical data is sometimes referred to as a *grouping* variable in that is allows us to "group" or break the data down into subsections or subgroups. Using gender, for example, one is able to examine the Total Number of Days Absent for females and males in the database. When we do this, we get two findings or results that we then compare and make our analysis: Who was absent more from school in the past year? From the data in Table 3.2, females had a total of 45 days absent, while males had 40. One of the interesting aspects about absenteeism by gender is that there is one male and one female who are making up the majority of absences. When you remove them from the data and recalculate the sum you find that absenteeism isn't that high among the remaining students. For the purposes of this book, we will refer to categorical data as grouping data or grouping variables. Other such examples of grouping variables are grade level (fifth, sixth, seventh), free or reduced lunch versus no free or reduced lunch, and students who had the new reading program versus students who did not have the new reading program.

The next level is ordinal data. **Ordinal data** is similar to categorical in that it still consists of categories, but now the categories have order, and there is meaning or purpose in that order. With categorical data it doesn't matter if you have male and female, or switch it around to female and male. The order makes no difference. But with ordinal data the order does makes a difference. One way to tell if data is ordinal is to see whether you can calculate an average or mean for the data set. If you can, then the data is not ordinal. For example, let's take the State ELA data in Table 3.3. The data reports students' scores as a Level 1, 2, 3, or 4. Typically, Levels 3 and 4 are considered a student performing at the level of proficiency. Because this is truly ordinal data (categories with order) one cannot generate a mean. All one can do is calculate the sum of students who are in each level and/or the percentage of students at each level.

Interval data is the next level up from ordinal data. Interval data is sometimes referred to as *continuous data* in some books and also called *scale data* in statistical software packages such as SPSS. Unlike ordinal data, interval data allows one to calculate an average or group mean for the data. In Table 3.3, the State ELA and math raw score is interval. For ELA the mean is 507 and for math 515.

Ratio, the last level of data, is similar to all the characteristics of interval data in that it is continuous data, but has a true zero. Granted a student might receive a zero on an exam, but that doesn't mean that there is no knowledge or synapsis reacting in the student's brain. A student might also attend zero days of the afterschool program, but again, this isn't a true zero. In education, we rarely have this type of data available to use. Common examples of ratio data are temperature, time, or speed. If a student were to be timed, zero seconds would be considered ratio.

Assessment Data

Keeping in mind that all data is categorical, ordinal, interval, or ratio in nature, it is also important to keep in mind the different types of assessment data found in school formative and summative assessments. When we talk about formative and summative, we are also adding in the element of timeline—when these assessments are collecting their data.

Formative assessments are used at various points during the learning process with the idea that the information will be vetted back into the instructional or learning process in time to make any needed changes so the learner can meet the designated learning objectives. Some common examples of formative assessments are: quizzes, tickets out the door, homework, and chapter or unit exams. AIMSweb, Fountas & Pinnell, and STAR Math are all examples of formative assessments. They are administered several times during the school year, and the data is used to provide interventions for students as the learning process is still occurring.

Summative assessments, on the other hand, are final scores meant to provide important information about students and their learning; however, summative assessments are permanent fixtures in that they typically become part of one's record or play a major role in creating a score that becomes part of the record.

Levels of Accountability

In addition to the levels of data discussed previously, there are also types of usages or areas for which data in education have relevance. These types of data are commonly found in the literature on school building improvement: accountability data, district data, classroom data, and individual student data. It is important to understand how each of these types of data work in the analysis process and what each one allows us to say about the data and the patterns found within each type.

Accountability data is data typically gathered on an annual basis, and its purpose is to determine how one, in this case a school, is performing against some established benchmark or level. While we might necessarily refer to it as accountability data, most of us are familiar with this type of data in that it is administered annually by the state and typically developed by, or in collaboration with, a state's education department. Accountability data is standardized in that it comes from an assessment that has been carefully designed and developed through experts and has established reliability and validity. While the assessment is given at the individual student level, the results are reported to the public in aggregate form, typically by grade level, gender, ethnicity, students with special needs, and by the percentage of students meeting and not meeting the prescribed benchmark. Accountability data, when provided in its raw data form, is typically considered interval data; however, once the data has been converted to scale scores, the raw scores are placed into designated levels (e.g., Level 1, 2, 3, 4) and are now ordinal in nature.

One of the main benefits of accountability data is that because it is a standardized measure, it allows a school district or school building to compare itself to others of similar demographics and characteristics. You often see the results of a school district in the newspaper, comparing the achievement of its students to the achievement of students in another district. A challenge with this data is that it often comes "too late" in that by the time this data is "cleaned" by the state education department and provided back to districts, many months may have passed. In addition, the data that the assessments provide is summative, making programmatic changes to the curriculum difficult.

District level data is data that also comes from assessments, but these assessments are either developed by the district and/or administered by the district in order to track the progress of students and their achievement (e.g., AIMSweb, STARS, or Fountas & Pinnell). One of the main distinctions between accountability data and district-level data is that with district-level data it is the district that determines what assessments will be given, when they will be given (i.e., timeline) and to whom they will be given (i.e., what grade levels?). Another difference is that unlike accountability data, student scores on district level assessments do not place school districts or buildings on lists of schools in need of improvement.

Classroom-level data is the next level of data. **Classroom-level data** is similar to district level in that it can be both formative and summative in nature; however, whereas district level data tends to be focusing on key content areas (e.g., ELA or mathematics), classroom data generally can focus on any content area. In addition, the number of different types of data collected under classroom level is much larger and diverse than under district level. Classroom data can range from quizzes, to unit or chapter tests, to homework, to grades on student projects, to participation in class, or "ticket out the door." Data from these measures can be formative and summative depending how it is used. Certainly, quiz grades are formative in that they provide the teacher with information about how students are progressing with learning the new materials, and there is ample time to make corrections or additions to their knowledge. A unit test is more formative, and while corrections to students' knowledge can certainly take place after a unit test is administered, the data (i.e., students' final grades) typically do not change.

Individual-student-level data is similar to classroom level in that any piece of data that is classroom level can be individual and vice versa; however, the key distinction is how it is analyzed. If data are aggregated for the unit quiz into a mean that represents that class overall knowledge, or the last three years of unit test scores for a grade are examined to see the trend, then this is clearly classroom level. But if one were to take an individual student and examine his grades over the course of the school year and how he did on quizzes in math in relation to performance on each math unit's tests, then this would be a clear example of individual student data.

ACTIVITIES

1. Review once again Table 3.4. Take a look at the different types of assessments that we use in schools that all generate data. Use the Types of Data Activity Sheet to create your own table of the different types of data you can think of in your building. Do this activity separately at first and then compare your results to other team members in order to create a comprehensive list.

2. Having a district level data person is a big benefit for a DAT. The ability to request that the data person select and manipulate certain types of data is critical to timely and productive DAT work; however, in order to better facilitate this process, the DAT needs to be able to request data in a clear, concise manner. Use the Data Request Activity Sheet to help you communicate clearly with your district data person. Use this sheet as a basis for developing your own that meets the unique requirement and context of your district and DAT.

SUMMARY

All of us, no matter how experienced, have some apprehension when it comes to data. You and your DAT are no exception; however, understanding the process that your DAT will use time and time again to gather, analyze, develop findings, and initiate an action is critical to the overall success of the DAT. It is also important to recognize that there are different types of data available to you. Data can be at different levels of importance: individual student, classroom, district, and accountability. It can be formative in nature, allowing further time and instruction to occur, or summative, defining a level of student's learning. It can be nonstandardized, such as a quiz or standardized like the California Achievement Test (CAT), allowing comparisons between students in your classroom to classrooms across the nation. A DAT may also have access to a data analytics person who is currently working for the district. This individual is a great asset to the DAT. It is highly recommended that the DAT establish a strong working relationship with this person along with a pathway for communication, which allows the DAT to make data and analysis requests.

NONTRADITIONAL TYPES OF DATA

Aside from different levels of data there are also nontraditional types. Some of these you may not have necessarily thought about. The following list shows some possible nontraditional types of data:

1. Attendance

2. Discipline incidents

3. Student surveys

4. Parent questionnaires, surveys, and focus groups

5. Student–teacher dialogue notes

6. Student mobility or transfer counts

7. Health information generally related to the student cohort

8. Community data such as unemployment numbers; family support needs information; mobility rates within the district, and to and from other districts

9. Library usage

10. Athletic team participation rates

(Continued)

(Continued)

11. "Question of the Week" responses from faculty

12. Title One information

13. Retention or promotion rates

14. Gifted and talented rates

15. Remediation numbers

16. Participation rates in all school activities

17. Disaggregation of all measures by subgroups (ethnicity, socioeconomical level, and ESL numbers)

18. IEP data: areas of common concern academically

19. Administration data on parent concerns, student concerns, and district input

20. Parent–teacher conference rates

21. Physical education data

22. Participation in school musical groups, drama groups, etc.

23. Afterschool program data

24. Cohort comparisons

25. Pre–K entry data

26. School lunch program participation rates

27. Guidance and social worker data: visit numbers and categories of concern

28. Parent contact logs (teacher logs documenting numbers and types of parent contacts)

29. Retiring or departing teacher exit interviews and surveys

30. Local college available data

31. Comparative data and information for similar schools within and outside the district

TYPES OF DATA ACTIVITY SHEET

Data Type	Type of Assessments: Formative/Summative	Standardized/ Nonstandardized	Types of Data

DATA REQUEST ACTIVITY SHEET

Name of Requester: _____

Contact Information: _____

Date Requested: _____ Deadline for Request: _____

Grade Level	Type of Data	Years

Other Specific Instructions/Additional Information:

How to Know
What Works

The DAT at Brower Elementary continues to meet and look at data; however, recently they have encountered another stumbling block about how to determine whether an improvement plan that they want to implement really worked or not. Let's take a listen to their conversation. . . .

Jack: *Well folks, we have the initial results of students' reading scores from the state exam, and it looks as though they have gone up by a few percentage points!*

Everyone cheers. A few members even clap.

Christine: *See, I told everyone that the new literacy curriculum was going to work. Teachers love it, and I have seen a difference in their classroom as we have gone in to observe.*

Klara: *I agree. I see a lot of the strategies that we taught during the professional development now being implemented by the teachers in their classrooms. I think that as far as instruction goes we have seen a big change in how teachers in the building teach literacy.*

(Continued)

(Continued)

Oliver: *That's great and all, and I don't mean to rain on anyone's parade, but how do we know that it worked?*

Laura: *I agree, couldn't the gains be due to a lot of different factors?*

Emma: *I have been hearing that the test was easier this year. I was on a conference call the other day, and many districts from all over the state were saying that their scores were up. Wouldn't that account for why the scores went up? Sorry....*

Oliver: *It is too bad that we can't have a control group, you know, like they do in research studies where one group gets the treatment and the other group doesn't and then we compare the results to see what group does better.*

Christine: *Maybe there is some way we can do something like that. Have some teachers take the professional development while other teachers do not, and then we compare their student results on the end-of-year exams to see which group did better.*

Emma: *That would be ideal, but don't you think there is a big ethical problem with that?*

Christine: *I know, the moment I said it I wished I could have taken it back....*

The group chuckles.

Jack: *There really is no way to have any sort of control group in schools when we are working so hard to try to make improvements. We can't deny a group of students a treatment that we have good reason to believe will be successful.*

Klara: *It's like the train has left the station ... we are all on the move, trying to make improvements as all students are trying to learn. It's not like we can do it over if we find that one group does better in fifth grade when we add this new curriculum. They have moved on to sixth grade, and it keeps going.*

Oliver: *School is a different situation than research, and that is just the way it is.*

Christine: *I know, so why did we have to learn all of those research designs in college? They may be fine for scientific studies that are controlled, but for practical application in a school building they seem pretty useless.*

Emma: *I just wish there was something else that we could use instead of research control groups that would serve as a framework for us to use.*

Jack: *I have been reading about cycles. . . .*

The whole group: *Cycles?*

Jack: *Yes, there are these things called cycles where you follow their steps. They don't create a control group—all students receive the treatment—but the cycle allows you to continually look at the data, make decisions about how it is working, make adjustments until you meet your goal, and everyone succeeds.*

Oliver: *How do we get hold of these cycles?*

Jack: *I've got some information about them. I will bring them in next week, and we can talk about how we might use them.*

Klara: *I'm usually skeptical about this, but it sounds interesting.*

Christine: *Now, why didn't they teach us about cycles in college?*

Again, everyone chuckles.

WHAT WORKS, ANYWAY?

As you can see from this latest conversation at Brower Elementary, it is difficult to know for sure if something works, or why something works. Understanding what works has been such an active conversation that there is an entire

site dedicated to just that: Established in 2002, the What
[r]ks Clearinghouse (WWC) is an online repository dedicated
to providing educators with effective programs in a wide variety of topics and areas (e.g., literacy, mathematics, behavior) that
have rigorous research studies from large samples to support
their use. While research shows these methods to be effective at
improving student achievement, the very act of implementing
such a model in your school building may not yield the same
results for a number of reasons. This is not to deter your DAT
from investigating the evidence-based programs highlighted
on the WWC. In fact, you and your DAT should certainly enter-
tain some of these programs and curriculums if they appear
to be aligned to the needs of your building. However, do not
expect to be able to implement these programs and magically,
overnight, with a wave of a magic wand have the results that
you so desire. Even the most evidence-based program will not
be successful if the setting you are implementing it in is not
"ready" to receive it and all that it requires.

For example, sometimes these programs need to have a
skill level that your current staff may not have. If the program
is not implemented to its full level, then the results are not
going to be at the level they were in the study. This becomes
one of the biggest challenges with school improvement in the
21st century—bridging this disconnect between the positive
results of a study and the capacity a building or district needs
to implement all of the technical aspects of the curriculum or
program, with evidence-based practices supporting it.

So, what is the alternative? Should schools use practices
that "match" their level of implementation capacity even
though these programs have not been shown to be successful
and are not evidence-based? Or should they implement the
evidence-based program incomplete and not get the results?
Again, this is a dilemma.

Experts in improvement suggest one of two approaches:

1. Implement the evidence-based program and move
   your building's capacity up to the level it needs to
   implement it correctly.

2. Take your current practices and modify them slowly until you get the results that you desire.

Either way, improvement experts in the field suggest DATs do this through what are called improvement cycles.

WHAT ARE IMPROVEMENT CYCLES?

Cycles, or **improvement cycles**, as they are referred to, come from a century of research and work in the improvement process (Langley et al., 2009). The idea behind the cycle is that improvement is not a stagnate or a one-time shot. Improvement, real improvement, takes time. The cycle, a continuous circle, allows a DAT to continue to explore, try new things, make adjustments, and become successful over time. Presented in Figure 4.1 is an example of such a cycle.

You may notice that there are no notations or steps on the cycle for you to follow (these come in the next chapters). You will also notice that the cycle not only continues for several loops but also progresses in an upward trajectory. This upward

Figure 4.1   Overview of the Improvement Cycle Process

Continuous Improvement

trajectory shows that as a group is "looping" through one cycle to the next they are also changing or modifying what they are doing (i.e., improving). This trajectory represents improving.

When we use cycles to help guide us through the improvement process, we determine whether the effort has been a success based on the final data that we gather. Again, there is more about this in the next chapters. The important thing to know at this point is that improvement doesn't come quickly, and as we are running through these cycles we are constantly making changes and monitoring data.

How Do Researchers Determine What Works?

One of the challenges that you and many of your DAT members may face is trying to break away from the "traditional" mindset engraved into you through taking research courses in college. You could see in the Brower Elementary conversation that DAT members like Christine and Emma naturally gravitated toward these types of designs when faced with the dilemma of trying to determine what works. We automatically default to the treatment control group design, whereby one group gets a treatment, the other gets what would have been normally offered, and at the end we look at results to determine if the results from the treatment group outperformed those of the control group. From the DAT members' conversation, you can see the ethical and logistical challenges that these traditional research designs present in an educational setting.

Pre-Post One Group Design

Now understanding why the control group design is awkward in education, and how its design is difficult to implement in an applied setting because it denies one group access to the intervention, we can move to an alternative approach. Another research design is what is referred to as the **pre-post one group** (see Figure 4.2).

Figure 4.2 Pre-Post One Group Design

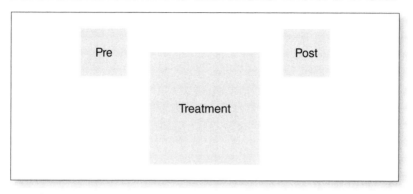

In this design, a premeasure is taken before an action is taken. The action might be an intervention, a new curriculum, or a set of new instructional strategies. Then the intervention is put into place. This is followed at the end by another collection of data. The researcher examines the change (if there is any) between the pre and the post. If there is a change, the researcher attributes this change to the intervention.

Many times in practical school settings, we use this design. We have scores on students at the beginning of the year, we implement a new program, and then gather scores at the end of the year. If there is a difference, we attribute the difference to the program. However, with the one group design we are not able to factor out what are called *extraneous variables* playing a role in this increase in student scores on the post measure. Let's take for example the test. Perhaps the year that you are implementing your new program the test is a little easier, hence why student scores improved. Another example would be maturation, the fact that students are naturally growing, developing, and therefore learning on a normal trajectory. Perhaps that plays a role in the post scores increasing over the pre? Without a control group in place, it would be impossible to factor out these extraneous variables from our equations. This design is often discouraged because with this design the researcher cannot say for sure if the pre-post change would have been greater if the participants were exposed to the regular intervention rather than the new intervention being tested.

While the cycles themselves are one group designs, the fact that one does not complete one loop of the cycle, but continues to loop through the cycle over and over, helps to extract these extraneous variables from the results. Take for example the test being easier one year. With looping through the cycles year after year, if in year one the test was indeed easier and scores were higher on the post-test, then in the second loop (year two) the test would most likely return to its "normal" level. If it was the test, then in year two student scores should drop back down and in theory "auto correct." If they do not drop and continue to show increases in percentages of students meeting proficiency, then it wasn't the test that was playing a role in the success, but the effective intervention that has been put in place. The continuous looping through the cycles will factor out all extraneous variables over time and help insure that what you are doing is indeed working. In the next chapter, you will be introduced in more detail to two improvement cycles: the exploratory and the confirmatory cycle (Creswell, 2015).

SUMMARY

As you could see from the opening conversation, it is difficult at times for DAT members to determine if something is indeed effective at improving learning and student performance. It is not a simple matter, and there are many ways to look at and determine success. Traditional research is useful in that it tells us what instructional methods are more effective than others. However, the research designs that researchers use to determine what works are difficult to implement. Cycles are one way a school can implement interventions and use these cycles to determine whether they are working. Cycles allow a DAT to focus on continuous improvement, modify issues that arise, and factor out extraneous variables over time as they continue to loop over and over through the cycles.

Following the Steps in the Exploratory and Confirmatory Cycles

Even though the DAT at Brower Elementary has had successes, the DAT that has formed at the middle school still struggles. Members from the elementary building attend the middle school meetings to try to support them and their efforts as much as possible. They have worked with the middle school team members to think about how to best use the exploratory and confirmatory cycles. They have collected data but struggle over what cycle to use and when, and where they should be collecting data. Let's listen in. . . .

John: Okay. . . . Well . . . we clearly have learned to ask the right questions. At least I hope we have. The proof will be if all this information helps us answer the questions we asked

(Continued)

(Continued)

　　　　and if we have a clearer picture of where we need to go and how best to get there. You all should have received copies of all this data in your email. I hope you've had a chance to look at it.

Sam:　Oh, I looked at it, all right, but jeez . . . there was so much of it. Who can make sense out of it all? I just feel overwhelmed.

Maria:　Yes . . . me too! It seems so hard to determine what data tells us what. There is just so much information now and no real way to organize it all.

John:　Well, I had the same thought, but I feel like we have never had so much information to help us with all of this and that the clues are somewhere in there if only we had a way to sort it all out.

Sam:　Yeah, trying to think back to my statistics class. Seems like that was in another lifetime! I do remember that there are different types of data. . . .

Jose:　Yes, and each type had a different purpose. We need to separate all this data out by type and purpose. I mean, I think I know what each type tells us, but I just can't remember all the technical terms and definitions.

Sam:　I did take an in-service class a few years ago which dealt with statistics and I know we need to label all this data according to whether it is summative or formative . . . but I hope there is some way to do it without all the technicalities of a statistics project!

John:　Let's hold on for a minute!! What we need is a way to look at each piece of data and put it in some form that will show us what it is trying to tell us. We don't need to label it . . . we need to organize it!

Jose:　You are both right I think. We need to sort and select all this data, but we need to break this task down into manageable pieces since there is so much of it. I suggest that we split up into teams of two or three, assign data to these teams, and have the teams decide how best to present the *data so it can help us. Some of the charts and tables and so forth that the data is in right now are just too hard to read and interpret. We need to do ourselves a favor and make all this data user-friendly!*

Maria: Okay, I'd be willing to look at all the student test grade data and see how it is presented. John, can you help me? We will figure out a better way to look at it so it can help us decide what to do next . . . I hope!

John: Sure. I just have a feeling that if we know what we are asking, we will know how to look at it in a more helpful format.

Sam: Oliver and I can take a look at all those parent surveys and try to sift out some trends and recurring themes.

Larry: Maria and I can collect all the data about the students—attendance, special education status, etcetera—and create a chart that will be easier to understand in terms of comparisons for each student. At least I hope it will!

Maria: Great. I do have an idea about that and would be happy to help out. We really need to make sense out of all this information, or we won't be able to use it in any meaningful way!

In the previous chapter, you were introduced to the two main data analysis cycles: exploratory and confirmatory. These two cycles are the core of this book, and in this chapter we will explain in more detail the different steps of each of these cycles. As you can see from the opening conversation, members are confused and overwhelmed with the data they have gathered. They wonder if they should have gathered it, as well as what to do with it. From their conversation, it is clear that they need a system or framework to follow. The exploratory and confirmatory cycles are the frameworks that would help them get on track and become successful. Let's begin with breaking down the different components of the exploratory cycle.

EXPLORATORY CYCLE

The **exploratory cycle** is one that is often a challenge for most DATs because as busy teachers and professionals, we do not allow ourselves the opportunity to explore, dig deep, make assumptions, make mistakes, and challenge the status quo. We always have to be right, and we always have to have all the answers. This is what makes the exploratory cycle such a welcome process. We can make assumptions, investigate the data, find that the data doesn't support our ideas or claims, and then make new assumptions based on what we have learned.

Step 1: Gather Data

The first step in the exploratory cycle is to gather data. Your DAT may want to spend some time brainstorming about the different types of data you may need. It is important during this step to not think about whether the data will support your ideas or not. Remember, this is the exploratory cycle, and as

Figure 5.1   Exploratory Cycle

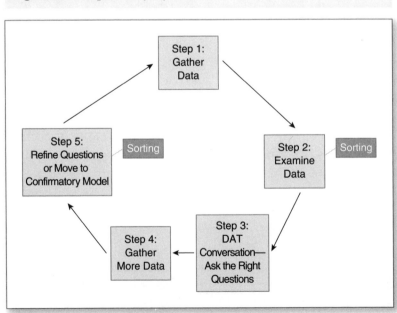

part of that cycle, assumptions fall to the side, and findings that until then have remained in the background come to the fore-front. Therefore, when gathering academic data don't exclude the idea of also gathering attendance data because these two are often associated with one another. Another example may be reading level data and math achievement data. At a quick glance the two different subjects areas may appear to have nothing in common, but in reality your DAT may discover they are very much related to one another. The bottom line here is don't limit your possibilities before you even begin by believing you know the answer to your question. Explore!

Step 2: Examine Data

There are many ways to examine data. Manipulating the data, reshaping it, and rearranging it visually are all ways or methods. In the first step, a DAT gathers data and then needs to examine the data. **Sorting** is one such way to reshape or manipulate the data to help us answer the questions that we have in the exploratory cycle. This technique reshapes or reor-ganizes the data so that it is in a different order. When apply-ing the exploratory approach to a data set, sorting allows the DAT to look for any interesting patterns. In the various elec-tronic spreadsheets that we have mentioned previously, one can select sorting as an option to manipulate the data.

We can choose to sort data in several different ways. The most common sorting approach is from ascending (smallest to largest) or descending (largest to smallest) when the data is in numerical form. However, one could also sort data by date, time, month, or year, as well.

Take for example the data set in Table 5.1. The data con-sists of test scores in mathematics for a single sixth grade class with 30 students. Also, to keep things simple, let's suppose that scores on the math assessment range from 0 to 100, with a score of 65 or greater being passing. You will see that in Table 5.1 the data are in alphabetic order by student's last name. This is most likely how it would appear in the teacher's gradebook. Take a moment to examine the data. What do you think about it? Can you draw any conclusions from it?

Table 5.1   Sixth Graders Test Data in Alphabetical Order

Student	Score on Math Test
Adams	91
Brown	55
Bryant	100
Connor	45
Crandall	89
Devon	45
Dowlings	99
Evans	54
Francis	89
Gram	91
Heller	59
Jackson	99
Kyles	100
Lyon	44
Michaels	100
Naples	58
Owens	90
Pratt	57
Quinn	91
Reeves	89

Unfortunately, in its current form, there isn't a whole lot one can say or conclude from the data set. We tend to look at the names and scores of the first couple (and last couple) of students. We might scan the data set to get a "feeling" for how the class did overall. But that is about it as far as patterns go. Let's now apply the sorting technique to the data set in Table 5.1 and sort the scores from least to most. See the results of this sorting in Table 5.2 below.

Table 5.2 Sixth Graders Test Data Sorted Least to Most

Student	Score on Math Test
Lyon	44
Devon	45
Connor	45
Evans	54
Brown	55
Pratt	57
Naples	58
Heller	59
Francis	89
Crandall	89
Owens	90
Quinn	91
Jackson	99
Dowlings	99
Bryant	100
Michaels	100

What patterns can you see now in the data for Table 5.2? With a passing cutoff at 65, you can more easily see that about half of the class passed while the other half did not.

Step 3: DAT Conversations— Ask the Right Questions

We all ask questions every day. Our profession is based on our need to know more and to do that, we need to ask questions: questions of ourselves, of our students, of our colleagues, of our community, and of the "powers that be." Asking questions is a skill learned early in life and used throughout our lives, but do we often take the time to take a critical look at our questioning skills? Are we always sure we are asking the right questions, and are we always positive we actually want the answers? Often, we telegraph the response we are seeking in the wording of our questions, and frequently we ask our questions of people who have no access to the answers we seek. Sometimes the question we pose doesn't accurately reflect the information we are truly seeking to acquire. Sometimes questions can be challenging and result in creating tension between those involved. We also face the danger of asking questions in a way that will solicit responses that leave us more confused than before we asked. Indeed, asking questions is not a simple matter. As you will see, a Data Team's ability to pose the right questions, specific to the task at hand, will require careful consideration.

Also requiring consideration is the usual process and order of posing questions. Typically, a question is asked, and (it is to be hoped) after careful consideration, responses are given or discovered. We would like to suggest that there will be times when the DAT needs to turn that process on its head and consider another, more effective order. Instead of the usual "question . . . evidence . . . answer," perhaps the team might consider the following sequences to be of greater value depending on their purpose at the time. Perhaps the new order might be "evidence . . . question . . . answer," or "answer . . . evidence . . . question." This sequence might be far more appropriate if the answer is synonymous with "goal." The DAT might choose to pursue their exploration using the "answer . . . question . . . evidence" sequence, which would be most appropriate when the right questions to ask are not immediately apparent.

When we construct a question from the data, the type of question is no different from the types of questions we have been posing for centuries: who, what, when, where, why, and how. Let's take "what," for example.

- *What patterns do we now see in the data in Table 5.2 that were not apparent when the data was in its raw version in Table 5.1?*

We clearly see two groups: a group who has passed the math test with a 65 or higher, and a group who have not passed the test (i.e., scores less than 65).

It is important at this stage to keep reminding ourselves that we are only generating *possible* explanations to these patterns. So, again, taking the math example and the pattern that we discovered (9 of the students not passing while the others did), let's apply the "why" question.

- *Why did 9 students out of 30 not pass the test?*

Let's take a moment to listen to the conversation of the middle school DAT as they discuss their explanations for the data. . . .

These nine students are not good at math. . . . why?

John: *Because they were having a bad day. Let's face it, we all have bad days. We wake up, things don't go as planned in the morning, and it sets the tone for the entire day. And remember, these are adolescents that we are dealing with; every minute of every day is a crisis.*

    John's idea is an interesting one; however, we don't know this from just one data point. Perhaps these students were just having a bad day. We all have them occasionally. In order to prove this idea, the DAT would have to examine math data for these students from over time, perhaps across the school year, to be able to get a better sense of how they are routinely performing in mathematics. If this is of interest to the DAT members, then this data should be requested and examined.

    The second explanation. . . .

Beth: *I teach that grade level so I am very familiar with that test, and I think the test is not appropriate because the reading level is not appropriate. The reading level is too high for some of these students, who could otherwise do the math calculations assessed by the math test.*

(Continued)

(Continued)

Beth's explanation for the data is a little more focused than, let's say, John's, but in order to determine if reading level is indeed the underlying culprit here, the DAT would have to request the students' reading level data and perhaps even a copy of the math exam so that they can determine its reading level. This may or may not be the reason, and it may only be a possible explanation for several of the students but not all of them. This might be a possible avenue that the DAT would want to explore further.

The third explanation is from Janice. Let's take a listen. . . .

Janice: *I know many of the students who didn't pass the test. I also know that they do not attend school regularly, so I think that they did not perform well on the math exam because they are not attending school regularly and therefore not receiving the instruction.*

Janice's explanation for the data is an interesting one. First of all, it is one that is more likely correlated with the literature on student attendance and performance. But let's say you weren't familiar with the research literature or didn't have access to such resources. How might you go about investigating this idea further? The most direct way would be to also examine the attendance data for these students and compare this attendance to the other students who did perform well on the math test. The question that you want to answer with this comparison is whether or not the nine students who did not perform well have proportionally the same absenteeism rate as the students who passed the math test. In this case, after the DAT had finished their deliberation, they decided to pursue Janice's idea about absenteeism and requested students' attendance records.

Gathering additional data is Step 4 in the exploratory cycle, as seen in Figure 5.1.

Step 4: Gather More Data

In Step 4, the DAT examines the additional data. Table 5.3 shows the data with students' total days attending for the school year included.

Table 5.3   Sixth Graders Test Data Sorted Least to Most by Total Days Attended

Student	Grade on Math Test	Total Days Attending
Adams	44	79
Brown	44	81
Bryant	45	60
Connor	45	75
Crandall	54	80
Devon	55	69
Dowlings	57	89
Evans	58	77
Francis	59	67
PASSING		
Gram	89	150
Heller	89	159
Jackson	89	150
Kyles	90	160
Lyon	91	158
Michaels	91	159
Naples	99	159
Owens	99	157
Pratt	100	159
Quinn	100	156
Reeves	100	161

When we add Total Days Attending to the table we can see that there is a clear correlation or relationship between students' performance on the math test and the total number of days. The more days a student attends, the greater the performance on the test.

Step 5: Refine Questions or Move to Confirmatory Model

As you can see from the process demonstrated in Steps 1 through 4, the exploratory cycle is one where your DAT requests data, examines the data, has a conversation about the data, reaches an assumption about the data, or requests more data until an assumption can be reached. In the example with students' performance on the math assessment, the DAT has reached a conclusion that attendance may play a bigger role in these students' low performance than the other ideas and variables that they discussed. The DAT may now decide that they want to move over to the confirmatory cycle. As part of this cycle, the DAT would want to develop an improvement plan (e.g., an intervention) that they would put in place to address the absentee issue that they have discovered. The next section of this chapter will provide an overview the different steps in the confirmatory cycle.

CONFIRMATORY CYCLE

Once the issue has been clearly identified in the data, a possible solution or "fix" is then implemented and tested. This testing process is the **confirmatory cycle**. The underlying purpose of this cycle is to gather data to determine if the plan made the desired improvements.

Step 1: Establish Baseline Data

As you can see in Figure 5.2, the first step in the confirmatory cycle is establishing baseline data. Baseline data is data that the DAT will use as a "guiding light" in order to establish a starting point for the data analysis process, and to test whether the improvement plan has been indeed a success. Originally, baseline data was used in single-subject research, particularly in the field of special education and individual student behavior therapy. Today, we use baseline data because it allows for a more applied approach to the improvement process.

Figure 5.2   Confirmatory Cycle

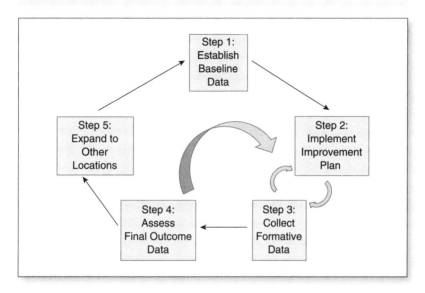

While there are no hard or fast rules for how much base-line data one should be using, it is advised that your DAT should try to use three to five previous data points. These data points that make up the baseline data could consist of a wide variety of denominations. For example, depending on the project, a DAT could use minutes, days, weeks, or years as baseline markers. For example, let's use four years of baseline data for fifth grade performance on the state's annual assessment in mathematics. Table 5.4 provides this baseline data.

Table 5.4   Stable Baseline Data for Fifth Grader Performance on State Mathematics Assessments

Date	% of Fifth Grade Students Proficient
2013–14	19
2014–15	22
2015–16	18
2016–17	20

In examining the baseline data found in Table 5.4, you can easily conclude that the baseline data is consistent from year to year. We often refer to this as the baseline data "being stable." In order to have the most effective confirmatory cycle, we want to make sure that we start the cycle with stable baseline data. Baseline data that is inconsistent or unstable will not be useful since one would not have a clear pattern in the data, and therefore would not be able to know where gains have been made, if in fact they had been. Table 5.5 is an example of where baseline data is unstable.

Looking at Table 5.5, you can see how difficult it would be to proclaim success if in 2017–18 30% of your fifth graders were proficient on the state's mathematics assessment. Would you compare it to the 11% from the previous year and proclaim a great victory? Or would you compare it to the data from 2013–14? This is the challenge when there is no clear, consistent baseline data present.

In situations such as this, where there is no stable baseline data, the DAT will have to try to find another data source that is more consistent. Also, if you examine the data in Table 5.5, you will see that a pattern does indeed exist. Every other year the data "dips" down. One could use this as a pattern, and then see if the pattern of every other year having this decrease once the improvement plan is put into place.

One of the best ways to use baseline data is to plot the data points visually on a line graph. While a more in-depth

Table 5.5   Unstable Baseline Data for Fifth Grader Performance on State Mathematics Assessments

Date	% of Fifth Grade Students Proficient
2013–14	29
2014–15	19
2015–16	30
2016–17	11

discussion of graphs can be found in later chapters, Figure 5.3 shows the baseline data from Table 5.4.

You can see in Figure 5.3 how much easier it is to visualize the data in baseline form rather than in a table. The unstable baseline data from Table 5.5 has also been posted in Figure 5.4.

Figure 5.3   Line Graph of Stable Baseline Data for Fifth Grade Students' Proficiency in Mathematics

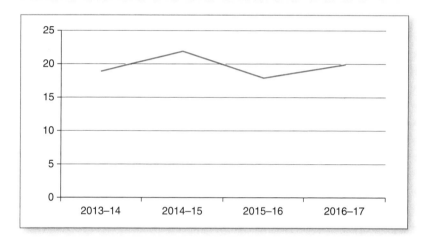

Figure 5.4   Line Graph of Unstable Baseline Data for Fifth Grade Students' Proficiency in Mathematics

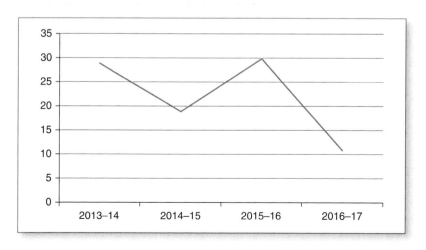

Step 2: Implement Improvement Plan

In this step of the confirmatory cycle, the DAT will work to develop an improvement plan. Again, this plan can take on various forms. It could be new curriculum, new procedures, or new ways of training teachers. A more in-depth discussion of improvement plans can be found later in this book.

Step 3: Collect Formative Data (Mini-Feedback Cycle)

As discussed in the previous chapter, the DAT should insure that there is a method of collecting formative data on the new improvement plan. While the final outcome data (found in Step 4) is important in determining if the plan has been a success, the formative data gathered in Step 3 is even more important. One would not want to implement a new program for an entire school year that was not producing the desired results, only to discover this at the end of the year. One would want to know this in the beginning of the year so the DAT could step back and develop ways to correct the issue. One of the challenges with formative data is that many times it is difficult to put something in place that is aligned with or predictive of the final outcome data. For example, fifth grade performance on the state's mathematics assessment is given by the state annually at the end of the year; it is impossible to use this as a marker for the formative data in Step 3. First of all, you would not have the test, and second, students haven't received all the instruction for the year, which means it would be impossible for them to do well on the exam (even if you had a copy) mid-year. In this case, the DAT would have to brainstorm about what alternative data they could look at to see if they were making gains with the new program and on track for success.

For this example, let's say that the DAT decided to use a district assessment given to students annually at the midpoint in the school year. The DAT would want to collect this data and examine this data as part of Step 3. However, if the district has implemented this formative assessment before, then the

Figure 5.5   Comparison of Baseline District Math Assessment
Data and Improvement Plan Data

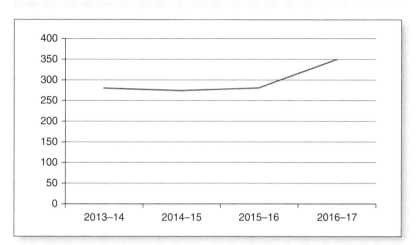

DAT would want to establish baseline data on this assessment for the last few years and compare the data mid-year with the improvement plan in place against the baseline data when the improvement plan was not in place. Figure 5.5 presents the district's baseline data for the last three years on fifth graders' mid-year assessments. Mid-year data from 2016–17 is the data for half a year implementation of the improvement plan.

In the example presented in Figure 5.5, the DAT might be excited because compared to the baseline data for the previous years, the average or mean scores for fifth graders are considerably higher. This would be considered a positive sign and one that would warrant no immediate changes to the plan. The plan should then progress to Step 4 to see if final outcomes are also achieved.

In this example, there was only one formative data source—the mid-year data from the district's math assessment. However, in reality one might want to incorporate several different types of formative data streams. In later chapters, we will provide more in-depth information about various forms of formative data and how to create some of the measures and tools to gather such data.

Step 4: Assess Final Outcome Data

This is the step that all members in the DAT have been waiting for: the moment they are able to see if all their hard work and effort paid off. In this step, the data collected as the plan has been implemented (e.g., post data) is compared to the baseline data. Take a look at the comparison in Figure 5.6. Pretend you are a DAT member. How would you interpret the results?

You most likely concluded that the scores for fifth graders in 2017–18 were notably higher than the baseline data. In fact, they had increased by 16%. While you enjoy celebrating your accomplishment with your other DAT members, you might also be wondering whether a 16% increase is enough of an increase or the increase could be due in part to other variables that are out there. This is a very good question and one that we should probably discuss. If you were feeling a little unsettled, you have good reason. You are correct. We do not know if some of the increase is because of external variables (sometimes called extraneous variables). These variables might include: the state assessment was a little easier this year, fifth grade students were a little more motivated this year than

Figure 5.6 Baseline Comparison to Improvement Plan Results for Stable Data

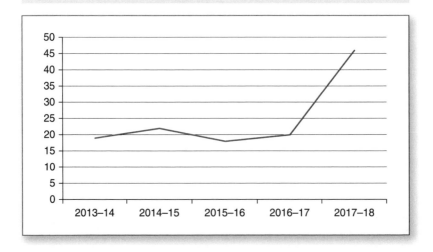

students from past years, or teachers put a little more effort into teaching because they knew their students' scores were being examined by the DAT. These are all valid and possible explanations that can't be ruled out. So how does a DAT factor these extraneous variables out? One way is through the use of the baseline data. Because there is the difference between what *had* occurred (baseline) and what *did* occur (final outcome data), we attribute that change to the improvement plan. Also, if we saw similar results with the formative data showing gains, this would also play into our belief that the improvement plan worked. Because it is impossible to say for sure that it is entirely the improvement plan, the best way to be sure is to continue to monitor the end outcome data each year.

Step 5: Expand to Other Locations

Another way to help support the idea that the improvement plan is truly making improvements is to replicate the plan in another location with similar need. The confirmatory cycle would have to be repeated in this new location. Baseline data for the new location would also have to be collected.

SUMMARY

At the beginning of this chapter, the conversation around the DAT table was one where DAT members were confused about the types of data they needed to collect and how they were going to use them. The exploratory and the confirmatory cycles provide DATs with unique steps to follow in order to execute each type of cycle effectively. The purpose of the exploratory cycle is for DAT members to investigate the data without a specific improvement plan in place. The exploratory cycle is designed to find a potential issue in the data itself through an ongoing cycle of gathering data, exploring the data, discussing with DAT members, and then gathering more data, and then repeating the process. Many times, the DAT will start with the exploratory cycle, only to follow it up with the confirmatory cycle afterwards. The confirmatory cycle is meant to test an improvement plan to determine if the plan is indeed successful and creates the desired results. Baseline data, a key component to the confirmatory cycle, is gathered and established before the plan is put in place. After the plan has been implemented, final outcome data is gathered and compared to baseline data to measure success. Formative data, gathered during the process to determine how the improvement plan is progressing, is another key component of the confirmatory cycle.

6

More Ways to Examine Data

The DAT at the elementary building has assembled once again to talk about data. Overall, the DAT has found the exploratory and confirmatory cycles when working with data to be of great value and find themselves at times flowing seamlessly from one cycle to the other. They have also been successful at introducing both the DAT at the middle and high school to these two cycles.

However, as part of this process, the team feels as though they could be working with the data in a more productive way. While they have been putting data into tables, Jack has taken it upon himself to search the Internet for YouTube videos about better ways to present and display data. Overwhelmed with the amount of information on graphing that he found on the Internet, Jack returns to share with the DAT what he found. Let's take a moment to join them and listen in on their conversation....

Jack: *Well, folks, as promised last week, I did a search on the Internet about best practices in displaying data.*

Laura: *And what did you find?*

Jack: *I found that I was overwhelmed with the amount of information that is out there. Some of it was too simple,*

(Continued)

(Continued)

> some way too complicated. It was difficult to find a happy medium and even more difficult to find something that was focused on the work that we are doing.

Emma: That always happens to me when I do any kind of searching on the Internet.

Jack: Don't get me wrong, I did find a couple of videos that are helpful and a couple of blogs that had some ideas that I think we can use.

Oliver: That sounds promising.

Jack: I think one of the most valuable blogs I came across talked about the use of line graphs. I could see taking our data and rolling it into line graphs, making it a lot easier to view and form a conversation about.

Christine: Oh, I remember those things from stats class. I had the worst problem trying to understand them half of the time.

Klara: I like them. I think any time you can graph something it makes such a difference.

Christine: Yeah, but aren't you a former math teacher? Math teachers love this kind of stuff.

Jack: I also found a site that talked about how to use line graphs to plot your baseline data and then the final outcome data when we are using the confirmatory cycle.

Oliver: Sounds a lot like the single subject behavioral modification work I used to do when I was teaching special education.

Klara: I know what you are talking about, Oliver. It does sound a lot like it.

Emma: Yes, but it's on a lot larger scale.

Jack: So, let's think about some of the data that we want to plot using a line graph and see what some of these attendance trends look like.

> *Emma:*   *Sounds fun.*
>
> *Christine:* *I can't wait. . . .*
>
> *Acknowledging Christine's sarcasm, the group laughs.*

As we demonstrated in the previous chapter, Step 2 of the exploratory cycle involves reshaping the data in a way that allows one to see patterns that were not evident beforehand. One method of reshaping data introduced was sorting, whereby the data was sorted least-to-most (descending order). In this chapter, you will be introduced to some more techniques that use the same sorting method, but instead of sorting by descending order we will use other types of variables (e.g., day or gender). In addition, you will be introduced to graphing. Graphing is another method that allows us to look at data differently. If you and your DAT members are able to master these two techniques, examining data will be an enjoyable and welcome event.

USING DIFFERENT VARIABLES TO SORT DATA

If you recall in Chapter 5, we sorted the student math score data from least to most. While this is a foolproof way to reshape data, sorting the data by descending or ascending order requires the data to be interval in nature. If you recall from Chapter 3, interval data is continuous. Examples of interval data are scores on an assessment, number of days, or number of referrals. However, what if you want to sort your data by a categorical variable? Remember, we referred to categorical data as grouping data. Examples of grouping data are gender, ethnicity, and free or reduced lunch.

Take for example Table 6.1. In this table, attendance is taken at the beginning of each day of an afterschool program. A Number 1 is used to mark the student as present or a blank to indicate that the student is absent. In addition, the data has Student ID and gender. Take a moment to review the data.

Table 6.1   Afterschool Attendance Data

Student ID	Gender	M	T	W	TH	F	M	T	W	TH	F	M	T	W	TH	F
432	M	1	1	1	1	1	1	1	1	1	1	1	1		1	1
50443	F	1	1	1	1		1	1	1	1	1	1	1	1		1
43294	M	1	1	1		1	1	1	1	1	1	1	1			1
67959	F	1	1	1	1	1	1	1	1	1	1	1	1	1		1
43444	F	1	1	1	1	1	1	1	1	1	1	1	1		1	
12349	M	1	1	1		1		1	1		1	1	1			1
943929	F	1	1	1	1	1	1	1	1	1	1	1	1			1
454923	M			1	1	1	1	1	1	1	1	1	1		1	1
54669	F	1	1	1	1	1	1	1	1	1	1	1	1	1	1	1
34597	F	1	1	1	1	1	1	1		1	1	1		1	1	
995543	M	1	1	1	1	1	1	1	1	1	1		1	1	1	1
12543	M	1	1	1		1	1	1	1	1	1	1			1	1
44534	F	1	1		1		1	1		1	1	1	1	1	1	1

Do any patterns emerge? (Note: Keep in mind that this example is just an excerpt from the real attendance data, which would be quite large because it encompasses the entire school year).

In its current form, it is pretty tough to see patterns in Table 6.1. But take a second to reshape the data, sorting this time by gender, and now refer to Table 6.2 for the results. In the second column, you can see females are all grouped together first, followed by males.

Now what patterns emerge? Let's take a look at day of the week by gender. When we do this, we see that males tend to be absent on Mondays more than females. We also see a little more clearly that some females seem to attend more on Fridays—the day when many males are present and partici-pating in the afterschool program. What questions might come about from your DAT with this new pattern? The most likely question would be what activities or lessons are taking place on Mondays and Friday for the afterschool program. Might this help explain this pattern? In this case, the DAT would want to check with the director of the afterschool pro-gram to see if there are activities that would explain this pat-tern. Again, to keep this example going, let's say that in fact there were different activities to help explain it. Let's say that on Monday there are academic tutoring sessions in ELA and mathematics, and on Fridays there are sports and free time in the gymnasium. This would certainly help to explain this pat-tern among males. In order to address this, the program would want to think about ways to take an accountable action based on the patterns discovered by the DAT. Perhaps survey-ing or conducting focus groups with participating students to see what they would like in the way of programming would be an effective next step. Perhaps females want to play sports on Fridays, but the sports being played are not something that they are interested in? In any event, follow-up data needs to be gathered in order to develop an improvement plan and implement such a plan in the confirmatory cycle.

Let's take another example to show just how powerful sorting the data can be for finding patterns. Table 6.3 contains archival data of a middle school summer program. This program

Table 6.2   Afterschool Attendance Data by Gender

Student ID	Gender	M	T	W	TH	F	M	T	W	TH	F	M	T	W	TH	F
50443	F	1	1	1	1	1	1	1	1	1	1	1		1		1
67959	F	1	1	1	1	1	1	1	1	1	1	1		1		1
43444	F	1	1	1		1	1	1		1	1	1	1		1	
943929	F	1	1	1		1	1	1	1		1	1	1			
54669	F	1	1	1	1	1	1	1	1	1	1	1	1		1	1
34597	F	1	1	1			1	1		1		1		1		1
44534	F	1	1		1	1	1	1		1		1	1	1	1	1
432	M		1	1	1	1		1	1		1	1	1		1	1
43294	M		1	1	1	1		1	1	1	1	1	1		1	1
12349	M		1			1		1			1	1	1		1	1
454923	M			1	1	1		1			1	1	1			1
995543	M	1	1	1	1	1		1			1	1	1	1	1	1
12543	M	1	1	1	1	1					1	1			1	1

Table 6.3 Database for Four-Week Summer Arts Program Unsorted

Student ID	Days	Grade	Ethnicity	Free/Reduced Lunch	Special Education
32123	2	7	W	No	Yes
35421	2	8	W	No	Yes
45432	2	7	W	No	Yes
53212	3	7	B	No	Yes
54766	17	8	H	Yes	Yes
56543	19	7	W	Yes	Yes
65432	7	7	W	No	No
87654	2	7	B	No	Yes
54443	14	8	A	Yes	No
56432	20	7	B	Yes	Yes
56543	16	7	A	Yes	No
67543	10	8	W	Yes	No
78732	17	7	B	Yes	No
78907	17	8	B	Yes	No
87876	19	7	W	Yes	Yes
454211	17	7	W	Yes	No
545444	20	7	W	Yes	Yes
567665	19	7	A	Yes	No
653212	16	7	W	Yes	No

ran in the summertime and provided a four-week arts camp for students at the school. Take a look at the data in the table. You will see that along with the Student ID, we have the total number of days students attended (i.e., 20 max. days), grade, ethnicity, whether the student is in general education or special education, and whether the student receives free or reduced lunch. As you probably know, these data points are quite common in school data and are generally reported publicly.

Do you see any patterns in the data? Probably not; again, in its natural form it's pretty difficult to see. Now let's take a few of the variables and sort the database one at a time. Let's begin with free or reduced lunch. Take a moment to examine Table 6.4. Do you see any patterns when sorted for free or reduced lunch?

Table 6.4   Database for Four-Week Summer Arts Program Sorted by Free or Reduced Lunch

Student ID	Days	Grade	Ethnicity	Free/Reduced Lunch	Special Education
32123	2	7	W	No	Yes
35421	2	8	H	No	Yes
45432	2	7	W	No	Yes
53212	3	7	B	No	Yes
65432	7	7	W	No	No
87654	2	7	B	No	Yes
54766	17	8	H	Yes	Yes
56543	19	7	W	Yes	Yes
54443	14	8	A	Yes	No
56432	20	7	B	Yes	Yes
56543	16	7	A	Yes	No
67543	10	8	W	Yes	No
78732	17	7	B	Yes	No
78907	17	8	B	Yes	No
87876	19	7	W	Yes	Yes
454211	17	7	W	Yes	No
545444	20	7	W	Yes	Yes
567665	19	7	A	Yes	No
653212	16	7	W	Yes	No

Taking a look at Table 6.4, we can see a pattern emerge with students who receive free or reduced lunch and those that do not. Overall, it appears that students who receive a free or reduced lunch attend the summer program more regularly than those who do not. Checking with the director of the summer program, the DAT learned that the program offers a breakfast, lunch, and an afternoon snack for all the students who attended the summer program, no matter what the student's financial situation might be. This information might provide some context to what the DAT members might be seeing in the attendance data.

GRAPHING DATA

Sorting is certainly an easy technique that you and your DAT can use; however, when a DAT has the opportunity to move data to another form of visual representation, it should take advantage of the situation. The next section is on graphing data and how you and your DAT can move the data you are examining in both the exploratory and confirmatory cycles to graphs.

Researchers, statisticians, and data analysts have long used graphing to represent data in ways to make it easier for people to understand. In order to truly facilitate deep and meaningful conversations around data, your DAT must first think about putting the data into a graph. A graph is essentially a "picture" that allows one to look at data with a different perspective, and with that new perspective see patterns that were otherwise not easily recognized in its previous form. In addition, graphs make data real. Staff who might otherwise dismiss data, now see the trends before them and quickly jump into action to brainstorm about how best to address it. When visually displaying data, it is important that data team members have a firm grasp of the different types that are available and understand the different types of data required to propagate them.

Types of Graphs

While there are many different types of graphs available, there are four common types most researchers and data analysts working in the field use. These three types of graphs are line, bar, pie charts, and tables.

Line Graphs

Line graphs, or *line charts* as they are sometimes called, are commonly used to show trends over time and show that there is a "connection" between the different data points. Not all data can be used to create a line graph. Typically, line graphs use data that is continuous. Going back to Chapter 5 and Figure 5.3, here is an example of a line graph that is used to plot the number of students who were proficient on the state's mathematics exam across several years in time.

While Figure 5.3 is a simple line graph that uses one line, it is perfectly acceptable to have a line graph that contains multiple lines. For example, if you were comparing attendance trends for middle school students, Grades 6, 7, and 8, a line graph with one line per grade across multiple years would be a very effective way to display the data for your DAT team to discuss. Figure 6.1 presents this data. What trends do you notice about the attendance data by grade that you would bring up at your next DAT meeting?

One of the first things you might have noticed is that the average attendance each year for seventh grade begins to drop in Year 4 in comparison to the attendance for Grades 6 and 8.

Line graphs can easily be created using the electronic spreadsheets (e.g., Excel) or statistical analysis packages (e.g., SPSS) mentioned in earlier chapters. If these two options aren't appealing to members of your DAT, you can always use the old reliable graph paper to create your line graphs. No matter what method you employ, there are a couple of key elements to line graphs that you will have to get a handle on in order to use them effectively.

Figure 6.1   Mean Attendance by Grade for Past Ten Years

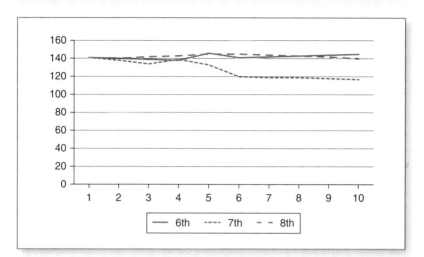

The line graph is made up of an X and a Y axis. The line along the bottom is called the horizontal or **x-axis**, and the line up the side is called the vertical or **y-axis**. The x-axis is sometimes referred to as the *independent axis* because it is independent of any variable; the y-axis is called the *dependent axis* since it is dependent on the x-axis. The x-axis may contain categorical data (e.g., years 2013, 2014, 2015, 2016) or interval data (e.g., number of days, number of referrals, number of students). The numbers on the y-axis generally, but not always, start at 0 in the bottom left of the graph, and move upward. Usually the axes of a graph are labeled to indicate the type of data they show. Take a moment to reexamine Figure 6.1. You will see that years as categories run along the x-axis, while average attendance days are represented along the y-axis. The grade level is presented by the lines themselves, and the ledger at the bottom of the graph indicates the grade levels depicted in the figure.

Perhaps your DAT wants to investigate the seventh grade data further. During your conversation, one of the DAT members suggests that looking at attendance by gender for seventh grade may reveal some interesting clues. Figure 6.2 presents this analysis in a line graph.

Figure 6.2   Seventh Grader Attendance by Gender by Years

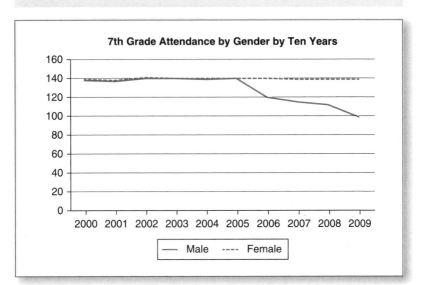

What do you see when you examine Figure 6.2? Most likely you notice that there is a difference in seventh grade students' attendance by gender: females have a higher level of attendance than that of their male counterparts. Again, this finding would create a healthy discussion for your DAT. Perhaps it is at this point your DAT decides to move from the exploratory cycle to the confirmatory cycle. In doing so, the DAT would put an improvement plan in place to address the attendance issue in seventh grade, focusing on all students at that level but particularly males.

No matter what the topic, you can see how valuable the line graph is in helping you and your DAT shape and reshape data during the exploratory cycle. The line graph is also a valuable ally in the confirmatory cycle.

If you recall from Chapter 5, the confirmatory cycle gathers baseline data prior to the implementation of the improvement plan and then later in Step 4 collects final outcome data and "judges" if a difference has occurred between the baseline and the outcome data, thus "confirming" the plan was successful. There is perhaps no more effective way to examine the data for the confirmatory cycle than by using a line graph.

In the next example, let's take four years of baseline data for student attendance. This would constitute baseline data in a confirmatory cycle. You can see in Figure 6.3 that attendance has dropped. Next, an improvement plan is put in place in Years 5 through 8. The improvement plan consists of adding two additional truancy officers to the school's staff. Currently, the building had employed only a part-time officer. These officers conduct home visits to the parents or guardians for the students who were flagged as missing school regularly. At the end of the plan, the data is examined again to determine if the plan was successful (Step 4 in the confirmatory cycle). Presented in Figure 6.3 are the results of the truancy officer improvement plan. Based on the line graph in Figure 6.3, do you think the improvement plan was successful?

While many of the examples in this book have shown baseline data that was stable over time, life is not always so nice and tidy. As mentioned in an earlier chapter, there will be times when the baseline data is not stable. How does our DAT determine if something has been successful with the final outcome data when the baseline data is all over the place, as in Figure 6.4?

Figure 6.3   Results of Truancy Officer Improvement Plan for Student Attendance

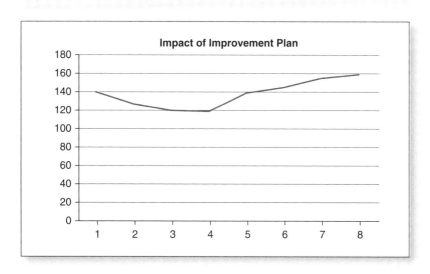

Figure 6.4   Unstable School Attendance Data for Seventh Grade

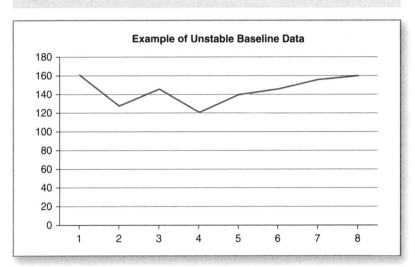

Now pretend you implemented a truancy officer program in Year 5 with the unstable baseline data (Years 1 through 4). Notice in Figure 6.4 that with the unstable baseline data, the average number of days attending for baseline is very close to the outcomes data for Years 5 through 8. How does a DAT make the call that the program was a success with this dilemma? In this situation, it is best to treat the results as tentative. It is also recommended that the program continue and that final outcome data in the confirmatory cycle be collected for several more cycles. In this case, the cycle would be school years. This will allow the DAT to adequately "test" the effectiveness of the improvement plan.

Continuing with this example, let's say we speed up time and collect three more years of additional outcome (four years total) data on the improvement plan. Let's take a look at how this all worked out in Figure 6.5.

In Figure 6.5, you can see that the unstable baseline data is a lesser concern when we have multiple years of final outcome data to examine. In this case, it is clear that the truancy officer has made a notable impact on the seventh grade attendance for both males and females. With this data, the truancy program looks like a success and it might be time, if

Figure 6.5 Four More Years of Outcome Data With Unstable Baseline Data

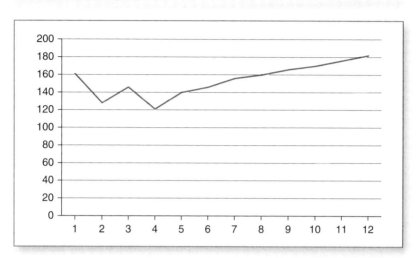

appropriate, that the DAT recommends the program expand to other settings within the district (Step 5 in the confirmatory cycle) to see if the same results can be replicated.

Bar Graphs

Unlike line graphs whose purpose is to show a connection between the data points, the purpose of the bar graph is exactly the opposite. **Bar graphs** display data points that are independent and not related to one another. Data used in bar graphs is typically referred to as categorical in nature. Examples of this type of data are when respondents are asked to report their technology usage as high, medium, low, or not at all. The levels of usage (i.e., low, medium, or high) are categories. You can see how this data would not be appropriate for a line graph. With categorical data, respondents have no other choice but to answer the question about technology use by checking off the choices. Analysis and summary of categorical data such as this focus on reporting either sums or percentages. For example, out of 100 people, 50 indicated that their usage is high, 30 medium, 19 low, and 1 not at all. Following along with this data, a bar graph would appear as Figure 6.6.

Figure 6.6   Bar Graph of Technology Usage in the Classroom

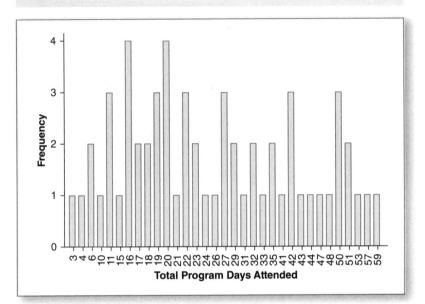

Pie Charts

Pie charts show how a whole is divided into different parts. Pie charts use categorical data. It is best to have approximately six to eight categories when creating a pie chart. You might, for example, want to show how a budget had been spent on different items in a particular year for a project. Figure 6.7 is such an example.

In examining the pie chart, you will quickly be able to notice that the majority of expenses has gone to salary (which makes sense), with the least portion of the expenses being attributed to supplies.

Tables

In the previous chapters, we have used tables as a method of displaying data. Tables are also another way to examine data for interesting patterns. Tables allow for multiple variables to come together, creating a juxtaposition with data between columns and rows. While there is no hard or fast rule, tables typically have a minimum of three to four columns and three to four

Figure 6.7   Example of a Pie Chart

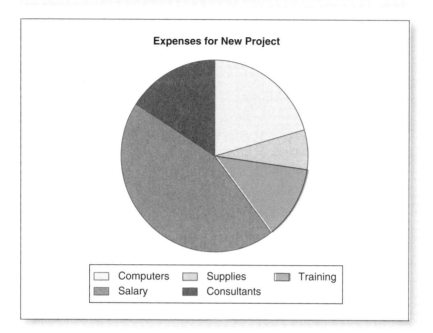

rows. This provides enough depth and breadth of information. Take for example Table 6.5. Notice all the information that is "packed" into this table. That is one of the reasons that many people use tables, because one is able to combine several types of data together and examine it in an easy fashion. This table examines elementary student performance by building by ethnicity for the 2015–16 state ELA assessment.

What patterns or findings can we derive from Table 6.5? One of the first things that you might notice is that more students at School B are performing at or above proficiency than the other buildings. School A, in fact, performed extremely low on the assessment, with only 10% of its total student body reaching or surpassing proficiency on the exam. In relation to ethnicity, across all of the buildings, it appears that whites outperform Black or African American students, and not economically disadvantaged students outperform those who are economically disadvantaged. What a DAT might be interested in doing based on the data in Table 6.5 is to examine these trends by building over the last five or six years. A bar graph or line graph could be assembled that would plot the percentage of students in each of the elementary buildings who achieved or surpassed proficiency on the state's ELA assessment.

In Table 6.6, you can see the percent of students proficient on the state mathematics assessment by district by grade level. This is an effective way of grouping data to look at larger differences and similarities. A DAT may find it helpful to start with this level of table initially, and then slowly extrapolate data from this table to look at in more depth during the exploratory cycle.

Table 6.5 Elementary Buildings Student Performance on State ELA 2015–16 (% Proficient)

	School A	School B	School C	School D	School E
Total	10%	80%	33%	31%	14%
White	5%	70%	44%	40%	15%
Black or African American	7%	15%	16%	21%	8%
Hispanic/Latino	3%	15%	17%	20%	7%
Not Economically Disadvantaged	9%	75%	54%	49%	21%
Economically Disadvantaged	10%	10%	20%	15%	12%

Table 6.6 Student Performance on Annual Math Assessment Across Different School Districts (% Proficient)

Mathematics Assessment	2010–11	2011–12	2012–13	2013–14	2014–15
District A					
Grade 3	39	39	8	19	16
4	44	47	22	18	28
5	43	35	10	15	13

Mathematics Assessment	2010–11	2011–12	2012–13	2013–14	2014–15
6	39	47	10	10	11
7	45	42	15	8	14
8	30	32	6	7	0
District B					
3	47	46	13	26	22
4	44	47	12	25	22
5	49	46	11	16	18
6	47	48	11	12	10
7	55	55	14	13	11
8	43	50	14	8	2
District C					
3	54	47	30	28	35
4	68	68	21	33	37
5	47	55	22	23	30
6	64	65	26	43	32
7	55	51	15	18	28
8	67	55	6	15	22
District D					
3	71	50	31	24	82
4	46	63	4	14	18
5	19	36	4	8	13
6	65	35	18	5	9
7	82	68	4	10	25
8	49	76	13	8	0
District E					
3	56	48	33	46	37
4	40	70	19	47	64
5	63	62	48	42	53

(Continued)

Table 6.6   (Continued)

Mathematics Assessment	2010–11	2011–12	2012–13	2013–14	2014–15
6	75	57	8	12	29
7	71	73	4	0	20
8	61	50	42	17	0
District F					
3	46	46	18	25	20
4	50	50	17	27	30
5	47	44	11	17	24
6	33	41	20	24	26
7	44	41	6	9	11
8	36	43	9	5	3
District G					
3	48	59	30	42	35
4	64	56	21	42	33
5	66	61	15	20	31
6	49	46	35	32	23
7	41	41	14	22	18
8	47	41	12	6	4

ACTIVITY

1. Graphs are all around us. Every day, we are exposed to different types of graphs without even realizing it. As a homework assignment, have members of your DAT be on the lookout for different types of graphs that they encounter throughout the week. They may find them on the Internet, in a newspaper article, or as part of a report. Have members bring copies of the graphs they encounter to the next DAT meeting, and for discussion, use the questions provided on the Graphs Activity Sheet for each of the graphs collected.

SUMMARY

Graphing is not only a way to present data, but it can be a way to foster rich conversation as well. There are several different graphs that may be useful. The line graph is a common graph that uses continuous data. The line graph shows that there is an overall connection to the different data points in the graph. Line graphs are particularly useful for showing trends or patterns in the data. It can be used in both the exploratory and confirmatory cycles. A bar graph uses ordinal data such as high, medium, and low or categorical data such as red, yellow, and blue. Pie charts use categorical data to show how parts or proportions fit together to make up the whole. Tables may be another good method for DATs to use when first starting to organize data. Based on the table, the DAT may decide to display the data using a line graph, a bar chart, or a pie chart to maximize the conversation among DAT members, as well as the greater school community.

GRAPHS ACTIVITY SHEET

Directions: Answer the following questions for the graphs collected from various sources.

1. What type of graph is it? ____line ____bar ___pie chart ____table ___other

2. What type of data does it contain (continuous or categorical)?

3. What is the overall purpose of the graph?

4. Are there any trends or patterns that are clearly visible with the graph?

5. Overall, does the graph clearly and accurately convey its message?

6. Other thoughts, comments, reflections:

7

Collecting Formative Data

By now everything seems to be going well with all three of the DATs at Brower Central School District. Each one has its individual projects and has been busy examining data provided by the district's data person. Everyone seems aware of the processes and steps in order to "sift" through the data and find interesting patterns that they then discuss in much more depth. All three teams have used both the exploratory and confirmatory models, and find that inevitably they go back and forth the between the two in order to fully accomplish what it is they want to do. All three DATs are also busy creating line and bar graphs, and pie charts to look for patterns. Both the elementary and middle school DATs are appreciative of the high school and the DAT members who provided the in-service on graphing for them. They believe it has helped their data analysis process and made them a much more effective team.

Despite everything going as planned, the teams have been encountering a new challenge to their work. It seems that in different situations the teams need more data than what the district is currently collecting or has in its archival data sets. For example, the middle school has been poring through assessment data in mathematics for the last five years, looking at the performance of students

(Continued)

(Continued)

in Grades 6 through 8 and seeing an unfortunate marked decline in performance on the state's annual assessment. To address this, a series of professional development trainings were introduced for the first half of the year. Teachers worked with math consultants on getting the most out of classroom learning and asking students the right kinds of questions to advance their learning. The consultants worked directly with the teachers in their classrooms, modeling and supporting the teachers as they worked on this new technique.

The DAT wants to look at *how* this professional development has changed the teachers' instructional practices. Initially they created a survey for teachers to fill out at the beginning and at the end of the professional development sessions. But DAT members really wanted to see if all of this training actually changes the teachers' practices. So they went in and observed several teachers as they were teaching and went back in after the training to see what exactly had changed.

DAT members liked the process. They like the idea of connecting the traditional professional development with the classroom observations. But in the end, they feel as though the data they collected from the observation could be better. They believe that they should have developed some type of form that they could have used in both the before- and after-classroom observations. Such a form would have allowed them to standardize the data collection among the observers. It would have also made analyzing the observation data a little easier. As things stand, they have only random notes each member of the team took when he or she observed. Reading over the notes at the meeting, they realize that their observational data is "all over the place." From this experience, they realize they need to do a little work and develop an observational form that will help them, and in turn, they hope this data will support all the hard work they are doing to improve student performance in mathematics.

THE ROLE OF FORMATIVE DATA IN THE CONFIRMATORY CYCLE

Previously, in Chapter 5, you were introduced to the five steps of the confirmatory cycle. Presented in Figure 7.1 is the

Figure 7.1 Confirmatory Cycle

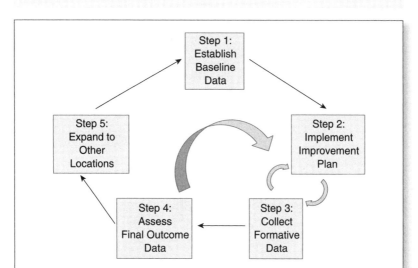

confirmatory cycle again in case you need a refresher. As you will see, Step 3 focuses on collecting formative data. This formative data is important because it determines whether the improvement plan put in place is working. Gathering the right formative data is often a challenge because is some cases it is not possible to gather the exact data that you will be using to determine your final outcome in Step 4. In many cases, we have to settle for collecting data that we believe is "related" to our final outcome data, in hopes that if we show improvement in this data we will also have improvement on our final outcome data. While it is impossible to cover all the possible scenarios where formative data would be used in the confirmatory cycle, it is possible to illustrate this type of data with a few examples.

USING CLASSROOM OBSERVATIONS AS FORMATIVE DATA

In some cases, it may not be possible to collect formative data that is as closely tied to final outcome data as in the previous examples. For instance, let's say that as part of an improvement plan teachers are trained in some new teaching strategies. The belief is that if teachers implement these teaching strategies, students' learning will increase in class and that the results should show an increase in the number of students proficient on the state's ELA assessment at the end of the school year. In this case, formative data that is collected might be observational in that DAT members go into the classes, observe, and see these strategies being implemented correctly. In order to gather such observational data, special instruments or tools first need to be developed.

Observational Protocol

An **observational protocol** is a tool researchers typically use to help collect and organize qualitative data. Observational protocols are generally open-ended, in that they allow the observer to write in-depth information, details, and descriptions about their observations. The observational protocol can be used in many different environments from classrooms to sports events. Presented in Exhibit 7.1 is an example of an observational protocol used to observe a typical classroom. Notice how the protocol collects specific information such as date, time, location, and name of observer. This particular protocol even provides a place for the observer to draw a rough outline of the setting. Next, the protocol consists of a series of open-ended items or questions. The observer responds to these questions using narrative to accurately describe the observation and the participants participating in an activity.

Observational Checklist

In addition to an observational protocol, there is also the opportunity to use what is called an observational checklist. An **observational checklist** is similar to an observational protocol because it is used to observe settings and participants in those settings; however, one of the main differences is that whereas the observational protocol allows observers to write full descriptions of what they are seeing, the checklist allows observers to check off only a score or number that

Exhibit 7.1   Classroom Observational Protocol

CLASSROOM OBSERVATIONAL PROTOCOL

About the Observed Classroom

School District: _____ Building: _____

Teacher: _____

Years of Experience in Education: ___1–5 ___6–10 ___11–15
___16–20 ___21–25 ___26–30 ___31 or more

Grade Level Observed: ___K ___1 ___2 ___3 ___4 ___5 ___6
___7 ___8 ___9 ___10 ___11 ___12

Name of Observer: _____

Number of Students in Class: _____
Number of Teachers/Support in Class: _____

Subject Area Addressed: ___Interdisciplinary ___Math
___Science ___English Language Arts ___Social Studies ___Fine
Arts ___Foreign Language ___Technology ___Business/Career
Education ___Family/Consumer Sciences ___Health/Physical
Education ___Other (please explain): _____
_____

Lesson Begin Time: _____ Lesson End Time: _____

Location: _____Classroom _____Library/Media Center
_____Lab _____Other (please explain): _____

Date: _____ Name of Observer: _____

(Continued)

(Continued)

About Classroom Management

Using the space below, please sketch the classroom layout, indicating the total number of students and teachers, the placement of equipment and people, descriptions and locations of materials or resources utilized, and other details that pertain to the lesson's implementation.

About the Curriculum and Instruction

1. Describe the instructional materials and equipment used to deliver the lesson.

2. If available, describe the instructional efforts that were employed before the lesson to prepare students for its content and activities.

3. Describe the lesson's learning objectives.

4. Describe the activities used by the educator(s) to meet the lesson's objectives.

5. Describe what components of formative assessment (from PD training) were used, if any.

6. Was any form of assessment present or evident?

corresponds with what they are observing. In other words, it quantifies qualitative observations through the use of scales.

Presented in Exhibit 7.2 is an example of an observational checklist. Compare it to the observational protocol in order to determine how it is similar in some aspects, yet different in others.

RELIABILITY OF OBSERVATIONAL DATA

When collecting observational data, it is important that the data you are collecting be reliable. This means that the data is consistently being collected. If you have two or more observers observing the same situation, let's say a classroom, and at the conclusion of the observations several of the observers report that the lesson they just observed was well done, while several others believe it is the worst lesson they have ever seen in their life, what does this mean as far as the data is concerned? Can we use this data? What value does it have? And most important, what is the truth. Is it the best lesson or the worst lesson of all time, or somewhere in the middle? In order to address this issue, **inter-rater reliability** is recommended. This is a technique professional researchers use to help ensure the quality of the data they are analyzing. It is also referred to as *inter-scorer reliability*. After the observation is completed the scorers convene and examine the scoring for each item on the observational checklist. Let's take the example again of observing a lesson in the classroom. Let's also suppose that one of the items on the checklist is pacing of the lesson and uses the scale presented as follows:

1 = Lesson is not well-paced

2 = Pacing off is at times

3 = Pacing is good

4 = Pacing is well-done

5 = Pacing is exceptional

Exhibit 7.2 Classroom Observational Checklist

CLASSROOM OBSERVATIONAL CHECKLIST

About the Observed Classroom

School District: _____ Building: _____

Teacher: _____

Years of Experience in Education: ___1–5 ___6–10 ___11–15
___16–20 ___21–25 ___26–30 ___31 or more

Grade Level Observed: ___K ___1 ___2 ___3 ___4 ___5 ___6
___7 ___8 ___9 ___10 ___11 ___12

Name of Observer: _____

Number of Students in Class: _____
Number of Teachers/Support in Class: _____

Subject Area Addressed: ___Interdisciplinary ___Math ___Science
___English Language Arts ___Social Studies ___Fine Arts
___Foreign Language ___Technology ___Business/Career
Education ___Family/Consumer Sciences ___Health/Physical
Education ___Other (please explain): _____
_____

Lesson Begin Time: _____ Lesson End Time: _____

Location: _____Classroom _____Library/Media Center
_____Lab _____ Other (please explain): _____

Observations of Off-Task Behaviors:

Off-Task Behaviors	Frequency/Number of
Students talking with others when they should be listening	

Off-Task Behaviors	Frequency/Number of
Students getting up and moving around the room during directions	
Students not following along during instruction	
Students fidgeting in their seats	
Students making noise that is distracting to instruction (e.g., tapping pencils)	
Students distracted by or interacting with others passing by in the hallway	
Students using computer, iPhone, tablet, and other devices when they are supposed to be listening to instructions	
Students writing or passing notes	

Now let's pretend that several members of the DAT rated the pacing of the lesson a 4 using the scale and several other members gave it a 1. This would not be the consistency one would want to see in order to establish inter-rater reliability. In the end, what is the truth? Was the class well paced or not? In this situation, the DAT would want to try and ensure that there was consistent scoring (or close to consistent scoring) for each item on the checklist. In cases such as the one presented here, when observers do not agree, a discussion usually ensues in order to determine what the observers were looking for exactly and how they came to their conclusions and scoring. In some cases, these discussions reveal things about the observations that shed some light on the situation. In some cases, one has to "rewrite" directions to the checklist in order to provide observers with consistency. An example of this might be observing "student off-task behaviors." One observer may count 5 off-task behaviors, and another might count 500! While this variance may seem extreme (and it is), what might be occurring is that one scorer (the one who counted 5) only counted a student who was tapping his pencil on the desk once while another scorer counted every time a student tapped his or her pencil. A discussion about this would eventually show the reason for the difference in total scores. Based on this, some directions would have to be put in place, and as a group the DAT would have to come to some decision about how it should be counting such off-task behaviors as they move forward and collect more data.

Another type of reliability that your DAT might want to consider establishing is **intra-rater reliability.** With intra-rater reliability, instead of trying to establish agreement between scorers one would want to establish agreement with the same scorer scoring at different times. Let's say that a teacher scored a student science project. Could the same teacher pull the same science project off the shelf a month later and score it and give it the same score? This should also be done if a lesson was videotaped and a scorer watches the lesson at two different points in time and scores it accordingly.

TIPS FOR CONDUCTING OBSERVATIONS

Here are some tips to keep in mind when your DAT is planning to do observations:

1. *Implement training.* It is important that you and your team members have a little practice with the observation protocol prior to actually using it. It is ideal if you have the opportunity to use it in a classroom that is not involved in the work that you are doing (so you feel no stress). After the observation the team can debrief and go over the items and their observations to see how similar people's notes are. If they are similar, then great! That's reliability. If they are not, why not? Take some time to further discuss among the members and try to determine why the inter-rater reliability was off. It might be because of the item on the protocol. If this is the case make sure the item is improved.

2. *Provide examples.* Put examples on the protocol as they are identified. It would look something like this: What are some of the instructional practices you are seeing in the classroom (e.g., . . .).

3. *Record sessions.* If possible, try to videotape a session. This is particularly beneficial in helping to further train DAT members. The video could be watched and scored by members who were not able to attend the observation. In addition, one could establish what is called intra-rater reliability. This is when someone would observe, then wait for a few weeks, and then watch the video and use the protocol again. Following this, the individual would compare his or her notes from the first observation to the second observation of the exact same lesson. In theory, the responses should be the same or similar in nature, because the lesson did not change.

4. *Account for observer effect.* Observer effect is something that happens when people are being observed and

act differently than they typically would. Educational researchers who employ observation as a method for data collection have to be keenly aware of this issue. For example, in a classroom, students might be better behaved and more attentive. Teachers may also prepare more for the lesson if they know they are being observed and will exert more energy and attention during the lesson. Observer effect is a phenomenon that happens to any profession that is being observed. It's natural. The reason to be concerned about observer effect is that if one is collecting data to see improvement, how does one know if what they are seeing is the improvement or those who are being observed are trying harder (which would look like improvement to the person from the outside)? Those who use observation would refer to this as *validity*. Is one measuring what one intends to measure? The only way to control or address observer effect is to stay in those settings for a longer period of time. If one goes in and observes for a short amount of time (e.g., one classroom period) the observer is most likely going to see only observer effect; however, if a series of observations are conducted (e.g., one per day over several days), by the end of the last few observations, observer effect should have subsided and the observer will most likely see what is more typical of the situation. Data should be collected only once observer effect has been controlled for.

5. *Align protocol with training.* If an observation protocol is created to examine the changes in teacher practices and this is based on a result of professional development, then it is important to carefully align the protocol to the professional development activities. In other words, one wouldn't want to teach people one thing and then go and observe something entirely different. In order to create an aligned protocol, it is recommended that those creating the protocol observe the

professional development sessions (or whatever the activity is) in order to fully understand the depth and breadth.

6. *Write quality items.* Make sure to write clearly and concisely. Try to avoid vague language. For example, if you want the observer to note the different types of technology, define technology. Do you mean computers or iPads or cell phones, or graphing calculators or abacuses? These are all examples of technology. Be clear. If you mean only computers, then say computers.

7. *Format appropriately.* Along with writing clearly, make sure that your final observational protocol is easy to use and visually appealing. Make sure that there is ample space for observers to record their observations. Use checklists for recording demographics such as location, grade level, age, or professional position. This will increase accuracy and not take too much time away from the most important part—the observation itself.

Ultimately, whether you are using observational protocols or checklists, the purpose of gathering this data is so that you and your DAT have formative data to gauge the success of the plan that has been recently implemented. If, for example, the DAT notes during the observations that the teaching strategies are not being implemented correctly (or not implemented at all), then the DAT will need to review this information, and an additional action will need to be taken. In the case of strategies not being implemented correctly, the DAT might suggest another training to help teachers with specific aspects of the strategies not being done correctly, or perhaps use an instructional coach to observe in the classroom and work directly with the teachers. The important thing to remember here is that even though this data is observational, it is very important to the cycle and the success of the improvement plan. Many times, we tend to concentrate only on the quantitative data—the test scores or the end results. In this case, if we don't see the strategies taking place, then we have not changed the learning environment and therefore will not see anything different in our final outcomes for Step 4 of the confirmatory cycle.

USING SURVEYS AS FORMATIVE DATA

So far, we have talked about numerical data (e.g., student attendance days), as well as conducting observations in order to gather necessary formative data. Gathering stakeholder perceptions using surveys is another avenue that your DAT may want to explore for collecting relevant and valuable formative data. While many people believe that surveys are simply putting some statements down on a piece of paper for people to answer, the truth is that in order to gather the right information, a certain amount of knowledge is needed about survey construction. While it is impossible to teach everything about survey development in a book such as this, we have tried to address some of the basic components for survey design to get you and your DAT started off on the right foot. We also suggest that if surveys seem to be a valuable tool for your DAT that you consider reading more about their development. There are entire books dedicated to the development, use, and interpretation of findings.

If a DAT finds it necessary to also collect information from surveys, they can be given at any time, but generally are administered before and after a workshop, training, or series of trainings. Their purpose is to document the trainings and receive feedback from participants.

As we can see from the Brower Central School District narrative, DATs may find it necessary to create a survey and gather data where there is no current survey being administered. Sounds simple, right? Unfortunately, developing a quality survey is a lot more complex than many people initially believe. The next sections will highlight some of the more important aspects that you and your DAT should keep in mind, whether you are designing the survey or analyzing survey data as part of the DAT efforts.

Likert-Type Scales

Scales are used to collect data for participants through the use of surveys. Typically, there is an item that presents a statement to the participant, followed by a scale or series of numbers. The most common scale is called the *Likert Scale*, a 5-point agreement scale developed by Rensis Likert (1903–1981). Likert's original scale consisted of the following points: (1) strongly disagree, (2) disagree, (3) neither agree nor disagree, (4) agree, (5) strongly agree.

Since Likert developed his scale, other scales have been developed and are often used. Here are some additional scales you may want to consider if your DAT is developing a survey:

- Always, very frequently, occasionally, rarely, very rarely, never (Note: frequency does not mean importance or quality. It means how many times one does something. Unfortunately, one can do something a lot with poor quality and very little meaning.)
- Very important, important, moderately important, of little importance, unimportant.
- Very good, good, barely acceptable, poor, very poor.
- Strongly disagree, disagree, slightly disagree, slightly agree, agree, strongly agree (6-point agreement scale).

Here too are some common things to keep in mind when writing survey items that use a scale.

1. *Make sure each item is a statement.* A question does not work with a scale. For example, an item that asks, "Are you good at using a computer?" is difficult to answer with "strongly disagree" and so forth. However, a statement such as, "I am good at using a computer," is not difficult to answer.

2. *Keep items simple and do not combine items.* If an item reads "I am good at using computers and robotics," and you are good at computers but not great at robotics,

how would you answer the item if you were given a Likert scale? Would you try to "average" your feeling on the two, would you go with computers and forget robotics altogether, or would you focus on robotics as you selected your response? This becomes a measurement issue. For example, if everyone circles "agree" but has different reasons or methods for combing the two experiences, it creates an invalid measure.

3. *Do not create an item that has a double negative.* To illustrate, let's take the item, "I agree that I have never been good at computers. 1=SD, 2=D, 3=SD, 4=SA, 5=A, 6=SA." Now pretend that you are indeed good at computers. How would you answer this statement correctly? Notice how it takes you a second (or two) to think about how to make your response accurately reflect your belief. The problem with an item that is worded this way is that many people will not take the extra second or two to do the "mental reverse" and might be more inclined to guess. Guessing is not something that those who design quality survey items want their participants to do. They want each item to be clear and concise, and they want to have confidence in the information those participating in filling out the survey are giving them.

4. *Highlight or bold key words in items that you want your respondents to focus on.* For example, if you are gathering specific information from participants that require them to keep in mind the activities they performed at the beginning of the school year, then it is important to bold that information in the item.

5. *Spell out all acronyms and abbreviations on first appearance.* It must be perfectly clear what you are referring to throughout the survey. Do not assume that everyone understands or knows common acronyms that are familiar to you and your DAT.

6. *Try to avoid using yes/no in a scale.* Whenever possible, you should try to use a Likert scale. However, yes/no

responses are appropriate in certain circumstances. For example, "Did you attend the computer training? (Yes/No) If no, please skip survey items 5–15 and only answer items 16–29."

7. *Try to avoid scales that have "I don't know" or "neutral" as possible responses.* While these responses might be useful in some specific situations, they generally do not provide the information that your DAT would be interested in when having to make a decision. Forcing people to make a decision either to the left (slightly disagree) or to the right (slightly agree) is better.

Other Types of Scales

Likert-type scales are not the only way to collect data with surveys. Another approach, a **checklist,** is a list or series of items that allows one to easily "check off." Here is an example of a checklist, asking respondents to "check the activities you participated in during afterschool programming."

Notice that the list also includes "other."

__Chess Club __Swimming __Arts & Crafts __Robotics
__STEAM __Sports __Discussion Club __Drama Club
__ Journalism __Fashion Club
__Other (please explain): _____

The purpose of "other" in this situation is to make the list exhaustive. Therefore, if someone did something that wasn't on the list, but related, this respondent can tell you what that activity or event was. Checklists are thus another commonly used device for gathering data from participants. The benefit of a checklist is that it allows participants to easily provide a wide variety of data; however, the challenge for using a checklist is that it doesn't allow one to get a sense of whether the activity or event was meaningful or beneficial.

Another alternative data collection device for surveys is the **semantic differential scale**. This scale provides two opposite ideas for participants to respond to a subject or topic.

Presented as follows is an example of a semantic differential scale for "technology integration into the classroom":

Not Important ___ ___ ___ ___ ___ Important

1   2   3   4   5

Not Necessary ___ ___ ___ ___ ___ Necessary

1   2   3   4   5

Difficult to Implement ___ ___ ___ ___ ___ Easy to Implement

1   2   3   4   5

Difficult ___ ___ ___ ___ ___ Easy

1   2   3   4   5

Similar to checklists, the semantic differential scale provides a quick, reliable way of ordering data. However, also like checklists, it does not provide anything in the way of depth of understanding. If, for example, someone was to indicate that it was "difficult to implement" technology, you wouldn't be able to really know why.

Understanding the "why" in survey data gathering is best done with open-ended items. **Open-ended items** are questions presented to the participants with no scale or possible solution. You might be more familiar with open-ended items as the question on a survey that asks to "please explain." Open-ended items are meant to be "free" in that they do not provide any hints or bits to persuade those filling out the questions in any way. Here are some examples of open-ended items:

What are three things or ways you benefited from the technology workshops and why?

Will you go about and implement what you learned at today's training? (Yes or No). If yes, how? And if no, why not?

What, if any, ways would you improve today's training? Please explain.

As you can see from the example, open-ended items allow for greater "conversation" or at least as much of a conversation one can have when using a survey. They allow a level of detail to be gathered that is not possible through the use of Likert scales, checklists, or semantic differentials. However, they, too, have their challenges. One of the biggest challenges with open-ended items is that they are not standardized in how they require participants to respond. Certainly, the item itself is standardized in that everyone gets the same item. But there is no scale or thing to "check off" in the response itself. People have to write their own response, and in doing so, may provide a wide variation of responses. In itself, this wide variation in responses is a good thing because this is the detail that one desires from open-ended items that cannot be achieved with a standardized scale.

PILOTING THE SURVEY

Before the survey is administered, it is a good idea to pilot the survey. A pilot is a sort of "dress rehearsal" where one would give a small group the final draft of the survey and ask those individuals to not only respond to the survey as though they were authentically taking it, but also provide written feedback and comments about what could be improved upon. In doing this, the DAT should provide pilot participants with extra paper to write their written feedback, since the margins of the survey may not have enough room to fully capture the depth and breadth of the feedback. After the pilot, the DAT should carefully review this information and make the necessary changes to the final survey form before it is administered to the other participants.

One of the real challenges when conducting a pilot is that many times one is dealing with a small sample to begin with. Let's say that you have 30 teachers participating in a professional development training on literacy strategies. How many from that population do you use in order to conduct an effective pilot? Experts in the field suggest that you don't use participants from this pool but see if you can find "similar" participants to pilot the survey with. For example, if the training was for fourth grade teachers, you could consider piloting with third or fifth grade teachers instead. Or perhaps you could find fourth grade teachers who weren't at the training. Granted, with both of these ideas, the teachers did not participate in the training, but they could still take the survey because they have similar professional perspectives, and in theory, they should circle "strongly disagree" with the items, since they didn't attend the training.

COLLECTING SURVEY DATA IN SCHOOL SETTINGS

Not only is creating a survey a challenge, but collecting the surveys from participants is also no easy feat. Presented as follows are some methods that you can use to collect surveys, including their benefits and challenges:

- *Mail out/mail back (SASE)*. This method, the traditional method for gathering survey data, allows respondents to take their time to provide accurate and thoughtful responses; however, this method is known for a low response rate (the number of surveys returned compared to the number mailed out). Low response rates can severely impact results, because survey administrators don't know if those who have responded represent the large sample. Electronic e-mails are essentially mail out/mail back and suffer the same fate of low response rates.

- *Fill out and pick up on site*. Also known as the workshop method, this involves handing out surveys and asking participants to fill them out and return them before they leave, or worse, get in line for lunch! While the response rates are very high with this method, the quality and accuracy of this data are debatable. Participants eager to get on the road, or eat lunch, tend to quickly fill out surveys using what is referred to as response sets: circling the same number on the scale for all items without carefully reading or reflecting on each item.

- *Drop box return.* Sometimes participants are given surveys by hand and asked to fill them out and drop them off later in a drop box, such as one in front of the principal's office. While this certainly gives respondents time to think and carefully respond to the surveys, having the data collection in such a "public" space could influence one's responses on the items themselves.

In the end, the answer is that there is no perfect method for collecting surveys. DATs who develop surveys and collect data using surveys will have to decide whether they want more accurate, thoughtful answers but lower or higher response rates and potentially less valid answers.

ACTIVITY

1. Apply the Creating an Observational Protocol Activity Sheet to a project that your DAT is currently working on. While you may not be needing to collect observation data, think about what observation data could be collected.

SUMMARY

While a large majority of the data needed by DATs to make decisions will come from the archival data collected by the district, there may be occasions when the DAT needs to collect some additional data. This additional data can come in the form of observation data and survey data. Observation data should be collected using an observational protocol or checklist. It is important for DAT members to carefully design the protocol and practices surrounding this type of data in order for it to be valid. Surveys are also challenging, and DATs should make sure that surveys are developed carefully before they are administered to participants. In addition to designing valid surveys, the DAT will have to think about the best method for collecting surveys, weighing the challenge between having high response rates versus more thoughtful valid responses.

CREATING AN OBSERVATIONAL
PROTOCOL ACTIVITY SHEET

Directions: Read the items below and respond accordingly. Be prepared to share this information with the other members of your DAT.

1. What areas/classrooms would you observe?

2. What characteristics would you be looking for in your observations?

3. Create a few of the items that you would use on your observation protocol to "capture" the characteristics you noted above in Question 2.

4. What challenges, if any, do you foresee in collecting this data? How might you go about addressing them?

Adding Parents
to Your DAT

If a DAT is to be truly successful, clear communication is key. As the Brower Elementary DAT welcomes its newest members, Jeanne Humbert and Helen Anthony, both parents of students in Grade 3, potential problems with communication can arise. The addition of these two parents is a positive development, and avoiding miscommunication pitfalls can prevent the team from encountering obstacles to success.

What follow are transcripts of Brower Elementary DAT meetings at which parent members are first welcomed onto the team. In all three scenarios, there is a communication issue, which has the potential to derail the process in some way. It is important to remind everyone of these potential missteps to avoid unnecessary problems.

In the first two scenarios, new parent members Jeanne Humbert and Helen Anthony are attending their first meeting. Having parents on the team can, and should, help the team to accomplish a great deal more. Parents can help in both the exploratory and confirmatory cycles. In the exploratory cycle, parents can ask questions that teachers might not otherwise think about, or they may ask questions from a slightly different perspective than teachers. The same is true for the confirmatory cycle. Parents can provide guidance in lots of the steps in this cycle, including the formative component where data is collected during the process. Parents' perspectives can be particularly beneficial in this process because they may shine a new light on the conversation that "illuminates" some variable or aspects of the situation (and a solution) to the situation that the DAT would have otherwise not developed.

Take for example the issue of student attendance at the seventh grade level. Perhaps the parents would have insight into why this is so. Is it development? Is it that many students feel the school isn't serving them? Is it that students and parents both believe the seventh grade curriculum is boring and not challenging for students? Whatever the issue may be, parent perceptions of that issue are critical and cannot be ignored. It is also important to gather information from parents about the solution or improvement efforts the DATs develop. Continuing with this example, do parents think a truancy officer visiting the homes of students who are chronically absent from school will be an effective method, or do they think that it will only increase the problem? What other methods might the DAT suggest to rectify the absentee issue of seventh graders?

INCLUDE PARENTS, RATHER THAN EXCLUDE THEM

Before the DAT can benefit from the expertise and wisdom of parents, it first must make sure that the conversation about the data is inclusive of parents and not exclusive. Educators are often guilty of slipping into the specific shorthand of our profession, assuming that everyone knows what these various terms and initial sets mean. We tend to speak in acronyms or in language specific to the methods and pedagogy of our profession, potentially leaving other stakeholders dazed, confused, and frustrated. They most certainly would be left feeling perhaps unprepared to participate beyond the bake sale, PTO, or parent conference level. Just imagine how you would feel at a doctors' conference, as initials and technical terms might leave you in the dust, assuming you do not have a medical degree!

1. *Avoid educator speak.* Here is an example of how the DAT might fall into this trap and possibly lose the benefits that these parent/stakeholders might bring to the table if they feel lost in our "lingo."

> Jack: Okay. Welcome, everyone. I'd like to especially welcome our two newest DAT members, Jeanne Humbert and Helen Anthony. Both are parents of students in our third grade, and both have expressed an interest in partnering with us as we seek to develop our plan to achieve our academic goals for the year. Today's topic will be how we can incorporate an examination of our third grade IEPs as they relate to our ELA proficiency scores and goals for next June. We know we need to move a percentage of our IEP students from the second quartile to the third quartile in order for us to achieve proficiency status on CCSS expectations. The EDOSA has provided some guidance that we need to review. So, let's get started. I'd like to list all ideas related to the IEP student achievement goals.

How much do you believe Jeanne and Helen got from this introduction? Unless they themselves are educators, it is unlikely that they would have anything more than a passing familiarity with what these terms and acronyms mean. It is also not likely that they would feel entirely at ease asking for clarification and explanation. Perhaps they might, but chances are they would either remain silent as passive participants or just stop coming to these meetings altogether. They would be made to feel lost, unprepared, and/or unqualified, and the DAT would then lose a participant and perhaps a vocal ally in the struggle for improvement.

2. *Avoid unclear expectations.* It is difficult to keep the DAT moving forward if they lose hope or misinterpret the expectations that have been set for them and for the students. If the expectations are not clear, the DAT members will participate in a more haphazard way.

Parents need to know what exactly is expected and required of them. They also need to understand exactly what the aims of the DAT really are. Here are some thoughts DAT parent members may have as they approach participation on a building DAT.

Jeanne (parent): *I'm going to my first DAT meeting. I've been thinking a lot about what Gabby the principal said. Sounds like an important job, but I just don't think I am up for it! I am far more worried about what she didn't say. Why do they need me? I don't know anything about data, and I am not a teacher. I'm willing to go and see what's up, but I'm really worried I'll be no help, and I don't want to be embarrassed and feel like I am in over my head. I love this school, and I really want to help. I truly do. I just don't know if I belong on this team. I love being PTO president, and I think maybe that is what I should focus on. I don't know about this DAT. I just don't know.*

Helen (parent): *I cannot wait to join the DAT. I have so many ideas, and I think the sky is the limit. I been doing a lot of reading about what other schools do, and I know we can make a plan that does it all for our kids. We need to make sure every kid scores at Level 4. After all, that's what the goal is . . . right?*

Well, both Jeanne and Helen are unclear about the expectations for the DAT and about their place on the team. Jeanne is insecure and doesn't have a clear picture of what a DAT is all about. She cannot imagine how she could possibly be of help, and she is fearful of being embarrassed because she doesn't think she knows enough. Helen thinks that the DAT is going to be the magic potion that succeeds where everything else has not—at least not completely. She also thinks that ideas that have worked elsewhere can be applied with equal success at Brower and that every child can score at the highest level. That may be true, but a lot needs to happen beforehand, and the DAT's role must be clear to her and to everyone involved.

In both cases, a short pre-meeting with Jack and a few team members would be helpful. The DAT members could lay out the tasks at hand and the expectations for the newest DAT members, answer their questions, and assuage their concerns. Getting these parents on the team in the earlier stages can help them learn more about data and its various purposes along with all of the other DAT members as they explore their new roles. Partnering parent members with a teacher on the team who can be their liaison would also be beneficial.

3. *Keep data relevant and not out of context.* Often the punishing aspect of data comes from the confusion about what it does and does not show—confusions about growth or proficiency, and success or failure. One of the pitfalls of miscommunication the DAT faces is that, often, people speaking about the exact same data believe it reveals completely different truths depending upon their perspectives and the availability of additional information. It is vital that DATs make it very clear at the outset of any data review what exactly the data type is, what it shows, what it does not show, and how it can best be used as the team develops its plan. When this does not happen, things often go awry. Witness the conversation on the Brower Elementary DAT as they set out to examine state test scores as to where each student's scores placed them on the continuum.

Jeanne:	*Well look at this! It is terrible. Only 20% of our students scored at Level 3 and only 4% at Level 4.*
Jack:	*True . . . that is this year's data, and it is the reason we have been identified as a school in need of improvement and been charged with creating the plan that will ensure better results.*

(Continued)

(Continued)	
Klara:	*It doesn't look good, and our results, as compared to Valley Elementary, indicate that we are truly a failing school at the moment. We have a long way to go.*
Emma:	*Well, this is the truth, and this is where we are, so at least we know how much we need to do in order to achieve at much higher levels.*
Oliver:	*It looks bad. 76% at Levels 1 and 2! Not good!*
Laura:	*True, but we at least know what our base is, and we can make some intelligent decisions on what the test results must show at the end of this school year.*
Christine:	*Well, how exactly are we going to figure that out? This only shows where we are . . . not where we need to be or even if it is possible to get to wherever that is.*
Jeanne:	*Wow, this is so confusing. I have no idea what you are talking about. All I know is . . . it sounds bad for our school. Seems like an impossible task to me.*
Helen:	*Well, this is worse than I thought. I am going to speak to a few parents and let them know how dire the situation is. I'll stay on the team, but this is one big job.*

The DAT is looking at proficiency in isolation. Before they can truly use it to their advantage, there is another factor that must be included, and that is growth. Yes, it is true that 76% scored below proficiency level, but is that better or worse than in previous years? Has there been growth? If so, how much? If there has been growth, then perhaps previous plans and efforts have been on target and must need to be enhanced or fine-tuned in order to move the process along more rapidly. If there has been no growth or even some decline, then the previous plans and efforts would need to be reviewed with additional scrutiny, perhaps with an eye to dropping those that seem to be counterproductive or ineffective.

This type of miscommunication can also leave parent members with false impressions about the school. If they feel that the task is too complicated, they might just withdraw. If they feel the need to share what misinformation they may have, the school will have to battle a more negative public perception along with all the other challenges at hand. All team members must always be clear on the purpose and definition of the data at hand. Miscommunication can and should be avoided. DAT members should always feel free to ask questions to ensure clarity of purpose and understanding.

PARENT VALIDITY

When we talk about measurement, we often use the words *reliability* and *validity* interchangeably. At meetings, particularly DAT meetings, someone will say that the state tests are not very reliable. However, when defined correctly, the state tests are probably very reliable. They, however, may not be valid in what they are measuring. Most times, DAT members will be really referring to validity but saying reliability. Because the two are related but very different from a measurement perspective, it is important that we define them both before going on and discussing what "parent validity" is in the way of data collection.

Reliability is consistency. When we think about a reliable friend we think of one that is consistent. The friend does what the friend says she will do, hence why she is a friend. Think of a measurement tool or an assessment in the same way. The test or assessment will give you the same information about a person over and over. For example, if I were to give your class a mathematics assessment on Monday and calculate a score for each student and then give the same assessment a week later (with the items mixed around so people wouldn't know it was the same test), I would expect each student to get roughly the same score on the assessment. Also, there would be no teaching or learning in between the two administrations. If there were great consistency in scores for each individual between the two administrations, we would refer to the test or assessment as reliable. So, when a member of the DAT is referring to the reliability of the state assessment (saying that it is not reliable), what he is really saying is that if you have the state assessment and it was administered again in a few weeks, students wouldn't get the same or close to the same score as they did a few weeks earlier. We all know that this is not true and that students would get roughly the same score. A student wouldn't be a Level 1 on the first administration and a Level 3 on the second administration; if so, the assessment would be unreliable and would be deemed unfit.

Validity is about measuring what one intends to measure. So, when a math assessment also has a large number of word problems that also require a high level of reading, comprehension, and logical applications, we say the assessment is not valid if we believe the assessment is only testing a student's mathematical ability. In this case, the assessment is not valid in that it is assessing other aspects of learning and a student's ability other than mathematics. In this case, if one was to "pull out" the mathematical calculations, a student who did not perform up to standard might do very well. In reality, most of the time when we are talking about assessments and testing students and these tests not truly reflecting a student's true potential, we are referring to validity, not reliability.

That said, let's take a moment to talk about "parent validity." As the above narratives between parents and teachers demonstrate, we all have different experiences and perceptions. This is what makes having a diverse group or mixed group on the DAT so valuable. Parents add a different perspective to the conversation. They are not in the school all day. They see the school from an outsider perspective, learning much of their information about the school and thus forming their opinions and perceptions about the school from the outside.

In order to gather valid information and data from parents, it is important to understand how parent knowledge and perceptions about the school are formed. This understanding plays out in the very questions and types of data you collect from parents. For example, let's say you are developing a parent survey as a second source of formative data; this will go along with your seventh grade attendance data that you are collecting and analyzing regularly in order to determine how your truancy officer improvement plan is progressing. The phrasing, words, and terms that you use in your parent survey are critical to the validity of the data. It is also critical to the response rate (the percent of surveys you get back) from parents.

If your DAT has parent members, then it is important to have the parents develop the survey right alongside the other members. If there is no parent representative on the team, then it is important for the DAT to pilot the survey with a small group of parents. This can done as follows: Set up a focus group of six to eight parents. Have the parents review the survey and provide feedback on it—its directions, questions, wording, and phrases. You will be surprised how many terms that you, from a teacher or administrator perspective, assumed parents would also understand. In the end, conducting a focus group will improve the validity of the data that you gather from parents and will inevitably end in a much more successful outcome for the entire school community.

TIPS FOR INCREASING PARENT DATA VALIDITY

- Do not assume that parents know all acronyms. Spell them out and define them.
- Do not assume parents know all procedures that a school has to undertake. In certain cases, an explanation of procedures should be provided.
- Do not assume all parents have high reading levels. Surveys and parent materials should be written at a seventh grade level (similar to most newspapers).

(Continued)

(Continued)

- Keep sentence structure clean and simple.
- Translate all surveys and materials into Spanish and other languages that are needed to include all parents.
- Think about the level of technology access parents in your school have. If you send a survey out electronically through e-mail or links to your buildings web page, you may be excluding the very population you want to gather this critical data from. Surveys may need to be sent out the old -fashioned way— through the United States Postal Service.
- If you are mailing surveys out in paper form, make sure to include a self-addressed, stamped envelope (SASE).
- Keep surveys short. Do not add unnecessary information or questions. Only ask what you need. Long, cumbersome-looking surveys deter many parents.
- Have a conversation with your parent DAT members about what they think are the most effective ways to gather data from parents.

ACTIVITIES

1. DATs can use the Defining Terms Activity Sheet to identify various terms and abbreviations that educators use every day; however, parents/guardians may be less familiar with these terms, and therefore we tend to alienate this group that we are trying so hard to engage with. Take some time with your DAT to work on completing this important task.

2. Parents invited to join the DAT can use the Identifying Issues Activity Sheet to help "bridge" the terms and abbreviations noted during the brainstorming activity with DAT members. In this activity parents/guardians will take these unfamiliar terms and work to develop them into terms that fit the parent/guardian perspective.

SUMMARY

Parents play a vital role in our schools, and therefore they also play the same role on DATs. Depending on the purpose of your DAT, you should consider inviting parent members to serve; however, in doing so it is important that you make sure your DAT is welcoming to parents. What we do as educators and how we communicate may seem professional and "normal" to each other, but it might not align to a parent's perspective. Keep technical perspectives and jargon to a minimum. Don't assume that parents understand the processes that we as educators use every day and take for granted. Also, be sure to allow parents the opportunity to express their opinions despite the fact they may not necessarily be aligned to the building's or school district's.

DEFINING TERMS ACTIVITY SHEET

(For Educators)

Directions: Read each item below and respond in writing accordingly. Be prepared to share your results with the other members of your team.

1. As professionals, we often use catchwords, abbreviations, and phrases that we understand but may not be apparent to those outside the immediate educational community (e.g., parents/guardians). Take a moment to brainstorm and list examples in the space below.

2. For each of the items you listed in Question 1, develop an explanation or definition that would be aligned to parent/guardian perspectives.

IDENTIFYING ISSUES ACTIVITY SHEET

(For Parents)

Directions: Read each of the items below and in writing respond accordingly.

1. What, if any, do you see as major issues in the school building? Please be as specific as possible.

2. From the items you listed above in Question 1, please describe in as much detail as possible how you would address these issues.

3. What data do you think would be appropriate to support these issues, as well as monitor their improvements and successes? Please list.

Continuing the Conversation Surrounding Student Data

It is the end of the school year, and the Brower Elementary DAT has gathered to discuss the state's ELA scores. All members of the team have stacks of printouts in front of them. The state's ELA scores have been broken down in many different ways for the team to look at and discuss. Prior to their meetings, team members received this data so they could prepare for joining the conversation. Overall, the results indicate that in some areas there were improvements and that in other areas there is still work to be done. Let's join the team and listen in to their conversation. . . .

Christine: *I know we have set up a process for how we explore data and have used it throughout the year, but this state test data seems a little different to me. It seems that when we look at data that is from this year and not archival, it requires us to ask different types of questions of the data.*

(Continued)

(Continued)

Oliver: I agree. I mean, I have questions about this data that we haven't touched upon before. For example, what are we supposed to do with it? Are we supposed to break it down to show that students still need work on certain concepts? Are we supposed to figure out what items are poorly worded and that is the reason students got them wrong?

Clara: And how are we supposed to use this data to try and do anything in the classroom?

Emma: And in reality, the school year is over and these students have moved on, hopefully, to the next grade. So, are we supposed to use this new knowledge for our incoming classes?

Clara: And our incoming classes might not have the same issues or gaps in knowledge that this class does.

Christine: See what I mean, I just don't know how we are supposed to use this data and what parts of it we are supposed to use. This is a little different than the trend data we have been looking at because there is no trend per se; the data is right here and now, and it is frustrating.

Jack: It's really all over the board, isn't it? What I thought we would do well on, we didn't and vice versa.

Emma: I'm shocked how many seventh graders missed question Number 7. I know that my students knew it, but the question is phrased strangely.

Clara: I know. I think it is the phrasing the threw many of them. Our students know this. . . .

Christine: What are we supposed to do in that case, for an item that lots of students get wrong but that we know is because of the wording of the question, and nothing to do with how we taught the content? Do I make curriculum changes based on this? Or what I know to be right?

Oliver: That is a good question. And one that we need to decide as a group. We don't want to be changing what we do when that isn't the problem.

As you can see from the DAT's conversation, end-of-year data for high-stakes assessments can be challenging, even for the most seasoned DAT. When your DAT comes together at the end of the year to examine data for these assessments, it is often difficult to determine what (if any) action should be taken. In this chapter, you will learn about some the techniques you and your DAT can use to examine this sort of data before making any decisions or taking any actions.

If you recall from previous chapters, most data derived from high-stakes assessment data is referred to as **accountability data**. This type of data is typically gathered on an annual basis, and its purpose is to determine how, in this case schools, are performing against some established benchmark or level. We refer to this as students who are proficient versus those students who are not proficient. While we might not necessarily refer to it as accountability data, most of us are familiar with this type of data in that it is administered annually by the state and typically developed by or in collaboration with a state's education department.

If you are using end-of-year data for your confirmatory cycle, then you would be using this data to determine whether or not your improvement efforts were a success. However, you might also want to examine your end-of-year data beyond the students' scores themselves and look for different types of data from the assessment. Here are some additional analyses that you and your DAT can perform.

LOOKING AT INDIVIDUAL ITEMS

When DATs examine data from accountability assessments, they often focus on individual items. One common method in this process is to look at those items that have a high number of students missing them. In the most recent Brower Elementary DAT conversation, Christine noted item Number 7 and the large number of students who missed this particular item. The real question when it comes to examining individual items is: why did so many students miss this item? In order to better understand why, the DAT should first take a close read of the item itself. Is the item poorly written or does it contain odd wording? If this is the case, it might be considered a "teachable moment" and teachers can consider adding this word to students' vocabulary or providing students with some strategies for "handling" poorly worded items. This strategy helps the DAT, and the teachers avoid unnecessarily changing pedagogy or instructional practices.

However, if the DAT examines the item and finds that it isn't the item itself creating the errors, but instead a concept central to the item, this indicates that a lesson was not taught or has not been taught in such a way. Some action is thus needed. The DAT will need to have a discussion as to what action can be taken to correct this gap in instruction for the future. Is professional development required in order to address an instructional issue or does some type of alignment need to take place so this topic is covered in the future?

In addition to looking at individual items, another pattern is to actually look at the pattern of items that students miss. For example, do students who miss item Number 7, also miss item Numbers 10, 13, 22, and 24? If so, and there is indeed a pattern, what could possibly be the underlying factor in that pattern? Could all of those items have the same or similar content knowledge needed in order to answer them correctly? This type of information would be beneficial to know, especially if your DAT wants to implement or recommend an action be taken to correct this finding. One pattern that you may notice is the disproportional number of students missing a single item.

ADDING OTHER VARIABLES TO THE CONVERSATION

While the DAT may see patterns in missed items across students, they might also think about adding other variables to the analysis. For example, in previous chapters, variables may be grouping variables (e.g., gender) or other variables (e.g., school attendance). Is there a relationship between students' level of attendance (e.g., low, medium, high) and the items that they missed?

Looking at District Level Data

The reality is that making changes, real changes, based on accountability data is challenging. District level data is a little easier to work with in some regard, in the sense that the data isn't collected at the end of the year but generally throughout the year. In general, this data, also known as *progress monitoring data*, also has a somewhat quick turnaround time because it is usually available a couple of weeks after the assessments are administered. Data that is given this way—in the beginning, middle, and end of the school year—can certainly be used to show where students are and where they need to be. Students who are not at a level by the middle of the year will need additional resources and support in order to get to where they need to be.

Many districts also try to use their district level assessments to predict how students will perform on the accountability state assessments at the end of the year. So, your DAT should begin to look at results for students on the district level and compare these results to the state level. If you have ordinal data (e.g., levels) for both your district and state accountability assessment data, then your comparison could look similar to what is shown in Table 9.1.

As you can see from Table 9.1, for the most part, district level performance at the end of the year is similar or aligned to student performance at the end of the year on the state's accountability measure in ELA. Once this has been established, then the DAT would want to look at mid-year scores on the district level assessment and compare these scores for students to end-of-year scores on the state accountability assessment. If they were indeed aligned, meaning that a mid-year district score would predict a student's success on the end-of-year state accountability assessment, then students who were not at that level on the mid-year should get additional support and interventions in order make improvements prior to the accountability assessment.

Table 9.1 Student Performance Seventh Grade ELA: District Compared to State Assessments (Levels)

Student ID	End-of-Year District ELA Assessment	End-of-Year State Accountability Assessment
04544	Level 1	Level 1
56543	Level 3	Level 3
65433	Level 1	Level 1
43276	Level 3	Level 3
32609	Level 2	Level 3
34321	Level 1	Level 1
7687	Level 4	Level 4
56789	Level 1	Level 2

TIPS FOR DIGGING DEEPER INTO END-OF-YEAR ASSESSMENTS

1. Look at items with a higher percentage of students who responded incorrectly.

2. Look at patterns among students and within student groups for highly missed items.

3. Look at items to which the majority of students responded correctly.

4. Try combing other variables when looking at patterns for an item (e.g., student absences).

5. Compare student performance on district interim assessments (progress monitoring) to performance on end-of-year assessments. Do they compare? Is there any predictability of the interim assessments to performance on end-of-year assessment?

6. Track an individual student across multiple years on end-of-year exams.

SUMMARY

Having conversations around data is essentially one of the main activities of a successful DAT. While many times DATs are looking for trends by examining archival data across multiple years, in some cases the DAT will be working with data from a most recent point of assessment. This time of data is known as accountability data. The purpose of this data is not to look for trends but to examine the data from the assessment and the assessment itself in order to ask effective and meaningful questions and to determine actions as a result of this process. One approach to examining this data is to investigate individual items on the assessment. Did large numbers of students across the building, across the district, or across the state miss certain items? If so, why? Were the items poorly written? If so, do we need to support our students further by teaching them reading strategies for approaching difficult or awkward text that they may be unfamiliar with? Was the content for this item taught? If not, how do we go about including it in instruction for the following year? These are just a few of the conversations a DAT can have around data that is derived from a most recent assessment.

Scaling Up Data

WHEN TO EXPAND TO OTHER LOCATIONS

Once a program or improvement plan has shown to be successful, the next question your DAT may have is: can this improvement plan work in other locations? This is a good question. Remember the example of the need for teacher training in ELA that was discovered by our DAT at Brower Elementary. You might also remember that this training did yield improved student scores on the state ELA assessment. So, let's say that you want to replicate the same training program in another school building at your district. Would you automatically get the same results? Let's also say that it is the same level building (e.g., elementary school) and you want to see improvement in the state ELA scores for the same grade level. One would think that this would be a pretty each transfer and all the DAT would have to replicate the same training and get the same results. However, there are some things that you will need to consider:

- *Student level.* Where are the students that you are trying to improve—what level? While there is clearly a need for more students to be reaching proficiency, it is important to try to determine that the students' needs in the new location are the same as the student needs at the original location (i.e., in our example, Brower Elementary).

Despite the fact student performance is low, it may be so for different reasons. One way to determine this is to have DAT members examine the individual items for students at the new location. Look to see the types of items that students missed and try to determine why. This information may give your DAT a better understanding or perhaps help identify what instructional practices need to be modified, and therefore better align the professional development training.

- *Teacher skill level.* While students may or may not have the same need in the new location, teacher level and instructional ability are also something to consider when scaling up a program. Are the teachers' instructional skills the same as in the previous location? If you recall from the example at Brower, the training need was based on the need that newer teachers to the building did not have the skills or experience yet to fully implement the ELA program with fidelity. If this new building had all experienced teachers who were implementing the ELA curriculum with fidelity and still had low student performance, then the reason behind this lower performance is different and therefore would require a different approach.

- *Characteristics of students.* In addition to variations in student and teacher skills levels, there are also the different characteristics of students in the building. Because of redistricting, demographics in the new building may be very different from those in other buildings. Your DAT would want to look at those demographic variables (e.g., percent of free or reduced lunch) to make sure that the expansion building was similar.

A MODEL FOR SCALING UP: PATTERNS IN THE DATA

Too often, a district will try to improve something in the district and in doing so implement the improvement plan across all buildings. We typically refer to this as a "cattle call" approach. One of the big problems with implementing this approach is that there is little time for anyone to learn anything from the process because the effort is being implemented at such a large level. It is virtually impossible to maintain or insure that it is being done correctly. It is also impossible to be certain that the approach will even work, and at the end of implementation the district may conclude that the effort did not result in any improvement— bottom line, nothing was improved and (worse) nothing was learned. Experts in the field of improvement note that it may take up to five to eight years to implement a plan, modify the plan, and see results from the plan as it has been continually "tweaked" through the exploratory and confirmatory cycles.

Recognizing this, the DAT interested in scaling up a project to another building should begin to lay out a multi-year plan in order to look at patterns in the data. For example, in School Building A in Year 1, after running through the exploratory cycle, the DAT implements the plan in the confirmatory cycle. At the end of Year 1, they look at the results and the results look promising, but they decide to continue through Year 2 with another round of the confirmatory cycle. At the end of Year 2, results are again what they were hoping for, so they continue on to another confirmatory cycle in Year 3, but they also decide to expand the efforts to School Building B. At the end of Year 3, the DAT wants to look at the results of Building B (one year of implementation) and compare those results to Building A's first year results. Are they similar? Does the DAT see the same things occurring in Year 1 of B as it did in Year 1 of A? If so, the confirmatory cycle should continue with Building A going into another year and Building B going into its second year. If results in Building B look good, then a new building should be selected and receive implementation of the program for the first time.

The idea behind "staggering" building level implementation of new programs to address need is just that—the ability to learn from the exploratory and confirmatory cycles, to keep things small so that they are manageable, and that correction of the model can be done swiftly and easily. If for example, at the end of Year 3, Building B did not achieve results similar to those of Building A after one year of implementation, this "staggered" process would allow the DAT to step back, examine the data, have many conversations as to why the results were not the same, modify the work that was being implemented, and monitor the situation looking carefully at the results in Building B at the end of the year.

Using Capacity to Scale Up

Another thing that your DAT should keep in mind when scaling up to another building or setting is to use all the knowledge that your DAT has gained during the exploratory and confirmatory cycles in your own building. This is valuable knowledge that can be shared with DAT members, faculty, and administration at the new implementation site. Take a look at the tips below when scaling up to another building.

TIPS FOR SCALING UP AND COLLECTING DATA

- Reuse materials and measurement tools that have already been developed. Surveys and observational protocols or checklists that were developed can be reused at the new location. There is no sense reinventing the wheel.
- Members from the DAT can visit and work with members of the new DAT. Sharing experiences, perspective, and stories is invaluable.
- Members of the new DAT can visit and conduct "walk-throughs" to see the plan in the established building that has been validated through the confirmatory cycle.
- Members of the new DAT can also look at the processes and patterns of their data in association with the patterns found in the previous building and use that in helping to determine if they are on the right path.
- Members of the new and old DATs can get together and help troubleshoot, especially if the new setting is not seeing the same results the other DAT had discovered.

SUMMARY

Once the DAT achieves the desired results through the confirmatory cycle, is it time to start thinking about expanding the plan to another site. While on the surface it might look relatively easy to expand to a new site, especially a building a few blocks away, the truth is that there may be subtle characteristic differences between the two buildings based on the students they serve and the teachers who serve them. It is not a recommended practice that a district implement a district-wide plan and implement the plan across all buildings at one time. This is referred to as the "cattle call" approach. The main challenge with this approach is that it doesn't allow the DAT to learn from the exploratory and confirmatory processes, nor does it allow the DAT to easily correct any problems that may arise and get the plan back on the pathway to success. A staggered method, where the plan is introduced slowly year-by-year into one new building at a time, is a better strategy for the DAT and the district. This staggered process also allows the DAT to share their knowledge, resources, materials, and lessons learned with members of the new DAT, faculty, and administration.

Epilogue

In September, the school year is off to a bright start at Brower Elementary. Several new teachers were hired over the summer, and they are enthusiastic to get involved in the building and school community. One of the new teachers, Erika Jackson, heard that the building has a DAT and that the DAT had been very successful throughout the previous school year. She was very interested in joining the DAT, and asked Jack. Jack told her how successful the team had been and a little about all the challenges they had to work out during the school year. Jack also told her that over the summer Klara had retired and so there was a vacant seat at the table. So, Jack invited Erika to attend their first meeting of the year.

As Erika makes her way to the library, she sees the last of the students boarding the buses. Soon the building will be quiet. When she enters the library, she finds it to be dark, except for a light way in the back corner. She makes her way past shelf after shelf of books until she comes to one of the back tables. There she finds last year's team: Jack, Christine, Laura, Emma, and Oliver. They are busy chatting and eating what look to be some delicious cookies that no doubt someone had made. They turn to her and introduce themselves and she joins them at the table. They begin to work.

Jack: *Our first order of business is to take a look at the student data from the mathematics assessment students took in the spring, and compare that to the results from the last couple of years. The question we are trying to answer today is: how are we doing?*

Christine turns to Erika.

(Continued)

(Continued)

Christine: Don't worry, just watch us and you will get the hang of it.

Laura: All this data stuff is easy once you see the process that we use.

Oliver: And don't worry about feeling beat up by the data because if they start to use the data to say we teachers aren't doing our job. . . .

Everyone at the table: We know, you're out of here!

References

Bernhardt, V. L. (2005). Data tools for school improvement. *Educational Leadership, 62*(5), 66–69.

Bernhardt, V. (2009). Data use: Data-driven decision making takes a big-picture view of the needs of teachers and students. *Journal of Staff Development, 1*(30), 24–27.

Creswell, J. (2015). *A concise introduction to mixed methods research.* Thousand Oaks, CA: Sage Publications.

Darling-Hammond, L. (2010). *The flat world and education: How America's commitment to equity will determine our future.* New York: Teachers College Press.

Langley, G. J., Moen, R. D., Nolan, K. M., Nolan T. W., Norman, C. L., & Provost, L. P. (2009). *The improvement guide: A practical approach to enhancing organizational performance.* San Francisco, CA: Jossey-Bass.

Thessin, R. A. (2015). Identify the best evidence for school and student improvement. *Phi Delta Kappan, 97*(4), 69–73. doi: 10.1177/0031721715619923

Spaulding, D. T. & Falco, J. (2010). *Action research for school leaders.* New York: Pearson.

Index

CORWIN
LEADERSHIP

Anthony Kim & Alexis Gonzales-Black
Designed to foster flexibility and continuous innovation, this resource expands cutting-edge management and organizational techniques to empower schools with the agility and responsiveness vital to their new environment.

Jonathan Eckert
Explore the collective and reflective approach to progress, process, and programs that will build conditions that lead to strong leadership and teaching, which will improve student outcomes.

PJ Caposey
Offering a fresh perspective on teacher evaluation, this book guides administrators to transform their school culture and evaluation process to improve teacher practice and, ultimately, student achievement.

Dwight L. Carter & Mark White
Through understanding the past and envisioning the future, the authors use practical exercises and real-life examples to draw the blueprint for adapting schools to the age of hyper-change.

Raymond L. Smith & Julie R. Smith
This solid, sustainable, and laser-sharp focus on instructional leadership strategies for coaching might just be your most impactful investment toward student achievement.

Simon T. Bailey & Marceta F. Reilly
This engaging resource provides a simple, sustainable framework that will help you move your school from mediocrity to brilliance.

Debbie Silver & Dedra Stafford
Equip educators to develop resilient and mindful learners primed for academic growth and personal success.

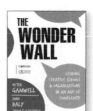

Peter Gamwell & Jane Daly
Discover a new perspective on how to nurture creativity, innovation, leadership, and engagement.

Leadership That Makes an Impact

Steven Katz, Lisa Ain Dack, & John Malloy
Leverage the oppositional forces of top-down expectations and bottom-up experience to create an intelligent, responsive school.

Peter M. DeWitt
Centered on staff efficacy, these resources present discussion questions, vignettes, strategies, and action steps to improve school climate, leadership collaboration, and student growth.

Eric Sheninger
Harness digital resources to create a new school culture, increase communication and student engagement, facilitate real-time professional growth, and access new opportunities for your school.

Russell J. Quaglia, Kristine Fox, Deborah Young, Michael J. Corso, & Lisa L. Lande
Listen to your school's voice to see how you can increase engagement, involvement, and academic motivation.

Michael Fullan, Joanne Quinn, & Joanne McEachen
Learn the right drivers to mobilize complex, coherent, whole-system change and transform learning for all students.

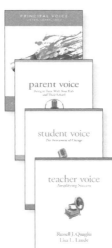

A SAGE Publishing Company

CORWIN HAS ONE MISSION: to enhance education through intentional professional learning.

We build long-term relationships with our authors, educators, clients, and associations who partner with us to develop and continuously improve the best evidence-based practices that establish and support lifelong learning.